START & RUN A
GIFT BASKET BUSINESS

Mardi Foster-Walker

Self-Counsel Press
(a division of)
International Self-Counsel Press Ltd.
  USA   Canada

Self-Counsel Press acknowledges the financial support of the Government of Canada through the Book Publishing Industry Development Program (BPIDP) for our publishing activities.

Printed in Canada.

First edition: 1995; 1996
Second edition: 1999; Reprinted 2001
Third edition: 2003

National Library of Canada Cataloguing in Publication

Foster-Walker, Mardi, 1952-
   Start & run a gift basket business/Mardi Foster-Walker.—3rd ed.

(Self-counsel business series)
Previous eds. have title: Start and run a profitable gift basket business.
ISBN 1-55180-503-0

   1. Gift basket industry—Management. 2. New business enterprises—Management.
I. Title. II. Title: Start and run a profitable gift basket business. III. Series.
HD9999.G492F67 2003   381'.4568   C2003-905062-9

Self-Counsel Press
(a division of)
International Self-Counsel Press Ltd.

1704 N. State Street
Bellingham, WA 98225
USA

1481 Charlotte Road
North Vancouver, BC V5J 1H1
Canada

CONTENTS

WORKSHEETS

SAMPLES

INTRODUCTION

The concept of giving gifts in baskets or in useful containers is not a modern-day phenomenon. It can be traced back to ancient times and cultures. For example, the Egyptians gave beautifully wrapped gifts of essential oils and perfumes; interestingly, today one of the hottest gift basket trends is giving aroma therapy products in decorative containers. The Haida Indians of the Pacific Northwest presented herbs or dried fish in beautifully crafted bentwood boxes, and the ancient Mayans gave gifts of food in colorful woven baskets.

The trend in gift packages today is very much the same as in ancient times. The container that holds the products must be useful and very much a part of the gift. Taking time to source out interesting and unique containers will set you apart from the more mundane and predictable gift basket competitors.

In modern society we give gifts for a variety of reasons, both personal and professional, and the potential for finding clients for a gift basket business is unlimited. The majority of people who send gifts want a unique and thoughtful present that will leave a lasting impression on the recipient.

This book is for people who want to start a gift basket company as a home-based business or in a rented studio/office space. It focuses on these venues because I do not believe that starting a gift basket business in a retail store is a viable proposition. Retail stores demand high overhead, long hours of operation, and a huge volume of sales necessary to be profitable.

Over the years, I have seen many gift basket retailers fail for these reasons. Those that do survive sell other products and gifts in addition to baskets.

A more likely route to success is to follow the trend toward non-retail, service-oriented businesses that simplify the lives of busy consumers. People will support and use your gift basket company for its convenience, quality, service, and reasonable prices. People want to send gifts that are special, yet most people who send and purchase gifts don't have time to shop and create something unique.

Many successful gift basket company owners start out by making baskets for friends and then realize they can develop their hobby into a viable and profitable business doing what they enjoy. If this describes you, then you'll find this book provides a helping hand as you take the entrepreneurial leap and plan for a profitable business.

You can start your gift basket business with little more than some working space and a few start-up items. There are very few equipment requirements for a gift basket company and it is possible to start a small, seasonal, home-based business with a very small investment. I know of one owner who operates her business during the December holiday season only, and she generates an annual net income of $20,000. On the opposite end of the scale is the entrepreneur who rents a studio/office space and runs the operation on a full-time basis. This book gives you the information you need to run a gift basket company on either a large or small scale. You have to decide what type of business you have the time and the money to invest in.

Gift baskets can be designed to fit any budget and suit any occasion, from small, inexpensive gift packages appropriate for the office or as hostess gifts, to large, custom-designed packages that reflect a theme, such as cooking, wine appreciation, golf, fishing, sports, or travel. The possibilities are endless and that is where your own creativity comes into play.

The art of designing and making gift baskets is a highly creative business and you need to have a good sense of design and an artistic nature to be successful. If you're uncertain of your talents in this area, but you feel that you'd be successful on the business side of the venture, you may want to consider bringing in an employee or a partner who is capable of handling the more creative aspect of the business.

You also need to keep up with the creative trends in the gift industry and the arts and crafts business. To give you new ideas and spark your imagination, you can spend time reading some of the many magazines available that deal with cooking, home decorating, and crafts. There are also successful television programs that feature decorating and craft themes. Visiting retail gift shops on a regular basis will also give you an idea of what trends, items, and themes are popular in the gift-giving market. Let your imagination run wild. For example, gift packages do not necessarily have to be in baskets. Some of the most innovative gift packages are in useful or unique containers, such as decorative file boxes, cowboy hats, tote bags, wooden toys, hat boxes, ice buckets, flower pots, or ceramic bowls. The possibilities are endless and your creativity is what will set you apart from other gift basket businesses. But creativity alone is not enough. You need to assess yourself and your life to see whether running a business is right for you, and this book will help you do that, too. A worksheet is provided in chapter 1 to help you focus on your strengths and weaknesses and guide you through the decision-making process.

Once you determine that the gift basket business is right for you, you can begin your adventure in this pleasurable and profitable line of work. The topics explored in this book will see you through those first crucial months and beyond and guide you to a successful venture.

Chapter 1
GETTING STARTED

a. Self-Assessment

What is it that makes one person succeed while another fails? While there is no stereotype of a successful businessperson, certain common characteristics can be found in those who succeed. For example, they are invariably hard-working, determined, resourceful, and capable of honest self-appraisal.

Starting your own business is risky, and you need to be clear on whether it is the best choice for you. You may already create gift baskets as a fun hobby, but turning your skill into a business is a very different venture. Examining both your strengths and your weaknesses gives you the chance to remedy the factors that may impede your success. If you don't manage time well, don't like to work alone, and dislike making decisions, starting your own business may not be for you unless you are willing to work on your shortcomings. You don't have to be perfect, but you do need to recognize and acknowledge your abilities and weaknesses before investing time and money in your gift basket venture.

To aid you in your self-analysis, Worksheet 1 is provided here for your use. It outlines some characteristics for success and asks you to evaluate yourself against them. Answer the questions honestly to determine how many success characteristics you already have.

This test will not definitively tell you what you should do, but it can help you engage in honest self-appraisal. A passion to succeed, an eagerness to learn, and an acceptance of responsibility can overcome any weaknesses.

No quiz, test, or questionnaire can definitively dictate to you what you should or should not do. Their value lies in helping you think by engaging you in honest appraisal. You are capable of capitalizing on your strengths and compensating for your weaknesses as long as you know what they are and if your passion to succeed is powerful enough.

Once you have determined that starting a gift basket business is the right venture for you, take some time to test your creative ability to make baskets. Purchase the materials to make two sample baskets, such as unique containers, basket stuffing, ribbon, cellophane, gourmet products, or other small gift items that reflect the look and theme that you have in mind. Experiment with making the baskets until you have a feel for what makes a visually and aesthetically pleasing package. Use these samples when doing your market research by showing them to family, friends, and, most important, to members of your focus group (see section **d.** later in this chapter).

b. Determining Your Market

The next step is to determine who your potential customers are — and if you have any. Do you know there are enough customers out there waiting to buy your gift baskets? Before you risk time and money and disrupt your life, you need to determine your market.

Many start-up operations are based solely on instinct and optimism. The enthusiastic new business owner may have only a vague idea about who the customers are or, indeed, if there will be any customers at all. Flying on blind faith, they rely on just plain old luck to see them through, and sometimes, it does just that. While every business needs a little luck now and again, banking on it is hazardous to the long-term health of your enterprise.

The benefit to the business you are considering is that gift baskets are not limited to the individual shopper. The corporate sector is rapidly becoming a major purchaser, and that means your potential market is very large. Gift baskets can be personal, professional, and designed to fit all occasions, tastes, and budgets. They are suitable for friends, family, co-workers, and clients. Often you will find that your corporate clients will also become your personal customers, and vice versa. If your initial sale is a success, you will have a loyal and long-term customer.

My own experience shows that repeat customers make up approximately 60% to 90% of my company sales. Think in terms of how much your average customer will be worth to you over the next several

WORKSHEET 1
SELF-ASSESSMENT TEST

Check the appropriate column for each of the following statements.
(N = never; M = most of the time; A = Always)

	N	M	A
1. I am a self-starter.	____	____	____
2. I am normally positive and optimistic.	____	____	____
3. I easily accept personal responsibility.	____	____	____
4. I have no problem working alone.	____	____	____
5. I am competitive.	____	____	____
6. I commit strongly.	____	____	____
7. I am flexible.	____	____	____
8. I am self-confident.	____	____	____
9. I relate well to other people.	____	____	____
10. I am a goal setter.	____	____	____
11. I am a creative problem solver.	____	____	____
12. I like to plan.	____	____	____
13. I am a decision maker.	____	____	____
14. I enjoy working hard.	____	____	____
15. I can tolerate risk.	____	____	____
16. I seldom procrastinate.	____	____	____
17. I am innovative.	____	____	____
18. I handle stress well.	____	____	____
19. I am independent by nature.	____	____	____
20. I am a logical thinker.	____	____	____
21. I am persistent.	____	____	____
22. I communicate well with others.	____	____	____
23. I manage my time well.	____	____	____
24. I have plenty of common sense.	____	____	____
25. I have the ability to think objectively.	____	____	____
26. I am in good health.	____	____	____
27. I like to learn new things.	____	____	____
28. I am realistic.	____	____	____
29. I can take criticism.	____	____	____
30. I am ambitious.	____	____	____

Now determine your score. Should you start your own business? Count your
Always and **Most of the time** answers as positive. If you scored

30 out of 30	You should be running General Motors.
26 - 29	You've got what it takes.
21 - 25	You'll do just fine.
16 - 20	Be sure you answered yes to number 14 and 27.
15	Questionable.
Under 15	Unlikely, but nothing is impossible.

years. It pays to cultivate customers into lifelong friends of your business, not only for the sales they will bring to your company, but by their word-of-mouth referral of new customers.

Make sure your gift baskets are easy to purchase. Most people are too busy to find the perfect gift. Once they have determined that you are a reliable company with high-quality product and service, they will use you as a personal shopping service. Your customers can describe their ideas, price range, and the interests and lifestyle of the recipient, and have the perfect gift sent without ever having to leave their homes or offices.

Study the buying habits of the consumers in your area when targeting your market. The key to your success is knowing what your potential customer wants and making sure you can provide the product. This will enable you to develop a loyal clientele who will then promote your services through word-of-mouth recommendations, which is the most cost-effective way to build your customer base.

c. Market Research

Market research will provide you with the relevant data to help solve or avoid marketing problems. Conducting thorough market research is the foundation of any successful business. The most prevalent and practical research method for a gift basket company is the focus group or survey. (See section **d.** later in this chapter.)

First you must research your competition. Any gift basket company that is doing serious business will be advertised in the Yellow Pages. Phone each company and keep notes on how the phone was answered and how your request for information was handled. Ask to have all printed brochures and price lists mailed to you. Choose the two or three companies that seem to be your biggest competition and order a gift basket from each one. Observe the quality and service that they are able to provide; this process will give you a good indication of what you are up against. Keep notes on all aspects of the transaction and use this information to formalize your own sales and marketing strategy.

Competition is not a deterrent to going into business. It is wise to know who your competitors are and where they are located so that you are on equal footing. Knowing your competition allows you to learn from them. What do they do right? What do they do wrong? How will you be better?

Market research helps confirm market size, minimize financial risk, save time, and point out where and how to sell your product or service. Researching your market can also uncover market segments that you may not have originally considered.

Not taking the time to do some basic market research can permanently forestall success. Obtain accurate demographics (population statistics categorized by age, income, sex, education, family size, etc.) as a credible base for your business plan.

Your market is that segment of the population that potentially may buy your product or service. Finding out who they are and where they are is what market research is all about. Market research is simply the process of collecting and analyzing information. The information gives you the basis for decision making. It will help you pinpoint advertising, develop a marketing plan, and sell your product.

Market research seeks out two distinct types of data:

(a) primary data collected for the first time by personal visits, telephone calls, or questionnaires, and

(b) secondary data from previously published material, such as government statistics and industry reports.

The steps in basic market research are discussed here.

1. Set a time frame for completion

Decide how much time you intend to devote to market research and stick to that time limit. Think in terms of normal working days and eliminate weekends. Do not get so caught up in doing research that it takes precedence over getting the business started.

2. Define both your primary and secondary needs

What do you need to know? By properly defining your needs, you can save valuable time and avoid having to cope with too much information. In order to give your business a realistic chance of success, and to have the information necessary to write a comprehensive business plan, you must define what primary and secondary data is relevant for your proposed business.

Primary data includes the number of potential markets, size of markets, size of total market, market trends, customers and target market, competitive companies, and market share. Secondary data includes demographics, industry outlook, growth potential, economic trends, population shifts, consumer trends, and relevant economic indicators.

For example, if your proposed business is located in an area with a cruise ship industry, you could use that as one of your potential markets and gather all relevant data. The potential market would be cruise ship bon voyage gifts. The size of the market is the number of cruise ships and passengers leaving the port yearly. Market trends would be a shift in average age of cruise passengers, more families cruising, etc. Customers and a target market would be travel agents who purchase gifts for their clients. Competitive companies are the number of other companies in your area that offer delivery of bon voyage gifts to cruise ships. The market share is the percentage of the cruise gift business you realistically think you could attain.

3. Allocate resources

Your resources are personnel and funds. If you are starting a business with a partner or if a family member is available, delegate tasks and responsibilities and try not to step on each other's toes. One person could make phone calls while the other goes to the library. The cash required should be minimal, but undoubtedly some will be needed. Government reports and publications may be necessary and many of them are not free.

4. Gather the data

Identify and contact the most appropriate sources for the information you need. Organize and file your research results as they accumulate. Don't keep unnecessary data, and do keep an eye on your projected completion date.

5. Analyze the information

Study the collected information as objectively as possible. Weigh your findings against your original idea. Does the data suggest a slight deviation from that plan? Does it affirm or negate your business premise? Cull from the data what is most pertinent to your planned product or service; date it and file it for future reference.

d. Gathering Primary Data

The most effective way to gather your primary data is to arrange personal meetings or a focus group with people who are potential sources of information. A representative from your local Chamber of Commerce, the head of a trade association, an executive from a hotel, the owner of a travel agency, and a corporate executive are a few examples. More than any other information-gathering activity, face-to-face meetings often lead to other important sources for data and will often establish business contacts that could be important to you in the future.

Always telephone well in advance to schedule the meeting. Know the name and proper title of the person you want to see and use it during your conversation. Introduce yourself and briefly indicate what you would like to talk to him or her about.

Prepare yourself for the meeting by reviewing the information you are looking for. Don't waste time or talk about your plans in too much detail. Write down information as the meeting progresses. Refer to your notes and ask questions to be certain that you get the information you came for.

Bring at least two samples of your gift baskets to show the quality, style, and various price points of your work. Make sure your questions are relevant to the person you are interviewing. Following are some questions for conducting a personal interview with a hotel sales and marketing executive:

(a) Do they now purchase gift baskets for their clients?

(b) How often do they purchase gift baskets?

(c) What type of gift baskets do they purchase?

(d) Are they happy with the quality of the baskets they purchase?

(e) What is the average price of gift baskets purchased?

(f) Do clients in the hotel ask them for referrals of gift basket companies?

(g) Do they have environmental concerns about gift baskets? (i.e., packaging materials or containers left behind for the hotel to dispose of)

(h) What type of products or packaging would appeal to them?

(i) What are their feelings about your gift baskets?

The more questions you ask, the better understanding you will have of your potential customers and exactly what they are looking for. After the meeting, review what you have learned, rewrite your notes, and file them.

e. Gathering Secondary Data

Identify and contact the most appropriate sources for the information you need. There are many sources of market information. They can begin with a telephone book and end with national computer data banks. Following is a partial list:

(a) The library: This should be your first stop when gathering any business information. Librarians are invaluable resources. Look through business and trade publications for trends and sales information. Often you can find market studies on file that can directly fit your needs. You can also locate census information and trade reports.

(b) The Yellow Pages: Your local telephone book can be a major resource. Study the classifications that list your competitors under the headings Gifts, Gift Baskets, Promotional Items, and Gift Packaging. How many competitors are there and do they use display advertising?

(c) Chamber of Commerce: This is an excellent source for all business information. If they cannot help you, they will direct you to someone who can.

(d) College or university business departments: Many of these departments offer extensive research help to the new businessperson. Occasionally they will take on the complete market research function for a company and use it as a teaching tool for advanced students.

(e) Government (particularly departments for small business development): In Canada, these departments are the responsibility of each province. The department that handles small business development can provide information on start-up help as well as federal programs that may be helpful. The Business Development Bank of Canada (BDC) conducts seminars on business topics which are very informative to anyone new to business. It also has books and pamphlets. There is a charge for most of these publications. If you do not have a BDC office near you, write to the nearest regional office.

In the United States, the Small Business Administration (SBA) offers publications covering topics such as budgeting, market research, legal structures, marketing, and financing. Call your local office and ask a counselor what is available.

(f) CompuServe Information Service: If you need demographics, this online computer service has it all. If you do not use a computer with a modem, you can use a computer search firm, but keep in mind that these services are not cheap.

f. Your Course of Action

At this point, you will have accumulated a lot of information, both first- and secondhand. What does that information tell you about your new business? Is the data leading you to think creatively about your new venture? If you are able to answer yes to the following ten questions, you are ready to follow a course of action leading to a successful new venture:

(a) Is there a market for your idea?

(b) Can you define who your potential customers are?

(c) Do you know who your competitors are?

(d) Can you see any advantage that your product will have over the competition?

(e) Do you know your competitors' prices?

(f) Do you know where your customers are?

(g) Are there enough customers to sustain your business?

(h) Do you know how to sell and market your product?

(i) Can you afford the costs of opening the business?

(j) Can you price your product competitively and still make a profit?

Once you can answer yes to all ten questions, the next step is to research a location for your new business and an operation site within that location.

Chapter 2
LOCATION, LOCATION, LOCATION

Once you have determined your market and are confident about your gift basket business, you need to find space to produce your product. This book is not intended for the businessperson interested in opening a retail gift basket operation. The two options covered in this section are finding and working from office/studio space and setting up a home-based operation.

a. Location Considerations

The two most important areas for consideration in choosing a location for your new business are:

(a) choosing a particular community, and

(b) deciding on a site within that community.

Opening a new business in a community with a declining, static, or small population would not be a wise choice. Choose an area with increasing and expanding population, permanent industry, upward mobility, and a minimum of season-related problems in the workplace.

When choosing a location for your new business, ask yourself the following questions:

(a) Is the population large enough to support your venture? Studies have shown that a population of at least 50,000 is necessary to support a gift basket business.

(b) Is the economic base stable and able to support a new business?

(c) What percentage of people are employed full-time?

(d) What is the average family income?

(e) Are new chain or department stores opening in the area?

(f) Are branch or head offices of large corporations or industries opening in the area?

If you are planning on running your business from your home, obviously you can't choose your space in the same way as you would if you are looking for space to rent or lease. But you should still go through the exercise of asking yourself the above questions, because if your answers don't support your business, you may want to rethink your decision of using your home as your base.

As well, even if you do decide to run the business from your home, you will still need to make sure that you do not violate zoning ordinances or rental agreements if you do not own your home. If you have space to run a home-based gift company, you should still spend some time researching the cost of office/studio space, which will give you an indication of what rental costs would be incurred if you ran your business in another location. Paying yourself the equivalent rent each month will give you a better indication of your profitability and the feasibility of future expansion.

b. Demographics of the Area

Determine the demographic profile of the potential customers in the community you are considering. Professionals and business executives will differ greatly in their purchasing interests from a working-class clientele, and urban city dwellers will vary in their interests and needs from potential clients in a suburban setting. Income, education, culture, religion, occupation, and upbringing influence the tastes and buying habits of your potential customers.

Consider the following factors when choosing a community to locate your business:

(a) Purchasing power or degree of disposable income

(b) Building activity and the range of housing

(c) Diversity of business establishments and industry

(d) Number of colleges or universities

(e) Cultural and leisure activities

(f) The age range of the population

A gift basket business is versatile and appealing to a wide range of clients. A gift basket service usually attracts customers who work long hours, have a steady income, and do not have the time to shop or create their own gifts. Generally, your potential clients will be well-educated, make average to high salaries, and be inclined to buy gifts that are creative as well as useful.

When you are satisfied that the community you have chosen can support your new business, it is time to choose a site for your new venture.

c. Leasing Office or Studio Space

If your dwelling is not appropriate for a home-based business, and you have enough capital to rent, you can consider leasing office or studio space. I have always leased space for my own company since my condominium is inappropriate for a home-based business. The advantage to leasing outside space is that you can set up a showroom and invite potential customers to visit and view your products.

Another option is to find another business to share space with, where you have a designated area to store inventory, assemble your baskets, and display your products.

Following are a few types of businesses that have good potential for space sharing:

(a) Gourmet food wholesaler

(b) Florist

(c) Artists and craftspeople

(d) Photographers

When leasing office or studio space, you must consider the issues of —

(a) proximity to customers,

(b) parking facilities,

(c) accessibility to loading dock or freight elevator, and

(d) storage and work space.

1. Proximity to your potential customers

My own office and showroom is located in the downtown business district of a major metropolitan area. I live within walking distance of the majority of my local corporate clients, and advertise that our showroom is open during the week for walk-in business. We also actively promote our business to the other companies in our building and have made many loyal customers who do not even have to leave their office building to receive our services.

Consider how close any potential office space is to your clientele. If you are hidden away in a back street, you won't attract walk-by traffic, and it will be more difficult to show off your product. You might find the monthly rental or lease rate lower in a less populated area, but those savings won't go very far if you can't attract customers because no one knows where you are. Make it easy for your customers to find you.

2. Customer parking facilities

Make sure you locate your office where there is plenty of free or inexpensive parking for the convenience of your clients.

3. Accessibility to a loading dock or freight elevator

When those big orders start to come in, you will be grateful for easy access to a loading bay or freight elevator.

4. Storage and work space

Make sure your office has sufficient space for storing supplies and inventory and plenty of space to produce your products. You can lease your own space in an office building, small business park, warehouse, or loft/studio space. These options are considerably cheaper than renting retail space, and you will still be able to receive customers. Choosing this option has the advantage of the professional image it lends to your company. Many large corporate accounts will feel more comfortable doing business with a company in an office building.

Another option is the "packaged office." This type of facility usually takes up the entire floor of an office building. Each company has one office space. There is one central reception area and a reception-ist who can accept deliveries, take messages, and for a separate fee perform secretarial services. These offices generally have a photocopy machine and fax machine available, which all the tenants share. You could run your business out of this type of space, but you would still have to make your gift packages elsewhere.

d. Signing a Lease

If you rent or lease space, you will need to decide what kind of lease agreement you are willing to sign. The longer the lease term, the lower the monthly rent, but you are responsible for the full term of the lease whether you are still operating the business or not. Some lease agreements will not allow you to sublet the space.

For a brand-new business it is probably best to take a one-year lease or month-to-month rent at a higher rate until you have ascertained how well your business is going to do. It also gives you the option of moving to larger premises if your first year of business is very successful. Always seek competent legal advice before signing any kind of lease agreement.

Before renting or leasing space ask yourself the following questions:

(a) Is the space accessible for receiving and shipping?

(b) Is there a loading bay and elevators?

(c) Is there sufficient parking for delivery trucks and customers?

(d) Are there enough electrical power outlets for your equipment?

(e) Is the lighting, heating, and air conditioning sufficient?

(f) Will your lease allow you to make necessary alterations, such as installing track lights and shelving?

(g) What type of advertising sign is allowable in your lease agreement?

(h) How safe is the area and the building?

(i) Will you be able to buy reasonable insurance against burglary and fire?

e. Shared Retail Space

I have said previously that I believe a retail gift basket operation is too high a risk. Retail overhead is very high, and it is unlikely that you could sustain a profitable business without introducing other aspects to your business.

However, sharing retail space with another business may be a viable option. Shared space can range from simply having your gift packages and brochures on display in a noncompeting type of business (expect to pay some type of commission for orders taken by the other business on your behalf), to actually running your operation in the same space as another business. If you decide to become involved in this type of situation, be prepared to pay a portion of the rent and other expenses. Have an agreement in writing with the other business owner, and make sure you know exactly what you are getting for your money. Before you agree to this type of arrangement, meet with the other business owner and discuss the following questions:

(a) How much space will be allotted to you for displaying your product?

(b) What portion of the rent will you be expected to pay?

(c) What other expenses will you be expected to share in?

(d) Will you be able to install your own business telephone line?

(e) Can you share the fax machine and line?

(f) Will you be allowed to have signs advertising your business outside and inside the premises?

(g) Is there sufficient storage space and work space to operate your business?

(h) Can you share other office equipment?

(i) Is the other business owner willing to market and advertise their business in conjunction with yours?

(j) Do the terms of the other business owner's lease allow for this type of sharing?

(k) Will you be covered by the other business owner's insurance in case of fire or theft?

Obviously, there are advantages and disadvantages to this type of arrangement, but if you find the right person and complementing business, it can be highly beneficial to both operations. One advantage is that the two of you can watch over the other's business when it is necessary to be out of the work place.

f. Seasonal Kiosks

During the busy December holidays, you may want to consider taking a kiosk space in a shopping mall, produce market, office, or public building. This can be as simple as setting up a table of sample gift baskets, handing out brochures, and taking orders, or a more elaborate portable structure that you have designed and built. If you run your business from your home, renting a kiosk can provide valuable added exposure to your business during this busy time. Even if you are renting office or studio space, which provides more exposure, you can attract new "walk-by" customers by setting up a seasonal kiosk.

However, keep in mind that renting a kiosk can be a large undertaking, and I do not suggest you try this the first year of your operation. Instead, during your first December of being in business, take a day or two to research locations for the following year. This will give you the opportunity to observe how others run this type of seasonal business and let you choose a location that seems to generate the most traffic.

If you decide that it is a viable option for you, start planning a year in advance. Find out who is in charge of leasing at the site you decide upon, and contact them in early January. Ask the following questions:

(a) How long is the period of operation?

(b) What hours are you expected to keep?

(c) What is the rent?

(d) What special licenses or permits do you need?

(e) What type of insurance do you need?

(f) What type of security is available?

(g) Is there a locked storage area available?

If you decide to try this type of venture, it should be because your business is successful and you are at a point where you can afford to hire someone to work the kiosk. If you cannot afford to hire a student or temporary employee to run the seasonal kiosk, then you should concentrate your efforts on running your already-established business from your home or office. The December gift-giving period is too important a time for a gift basket company to risk having you away from the office or workshop.

If you decide to have a custom-made kiosk, have a cart on wheels built. This can be rolled away at night and put in a secured area. It will also be useful throughout the year because you can use it for display and at craft shows and trade fairs. Depending on how elaborate you want to get, you should be able to have a mobile cart designed and built for around $1,000. Don't forget to have a professionally designed sign made so your potential customers know what you are selling.

g. The Home-Based Business

The home-based business is a unique blend of family, skills, and lifestyle. To make the blend rich and prosperous, each must be considered independently. Will your gift basket business suit your home environment? Do you have sufficient space to work undisturbed? Does working from home suit your personal style?

Think carefully.

1. The business and your home

Ideally, you have a separate room where, at the end of the day, you can shut the door (and lock it from inquisitive children). There needs to be enough space for supplies, inventory, and record keeping. Walk through your home with new eyes and visualize where you could set up a place of business. Many residential floor plans make no allowances for workspace.

See if there is enough privacy. You need to work uninterrupted. Figure out where your business telephone will be. You must be able to have uninterrupted telephone conversations — they are essential to your business. A door ensures that you can separate your business from housework.

Think about noise. Will your business create intolerable noise or will other people's noise be intolerable for your business? Most inside doors are hollow and easily allow sound to pass through. If there is potential friction over noise, it may be worthwhile to install a solid core door.

Your business should be compatible with the area you live in and cause no annoyance to your neighbors. Some area residents have closed down home-based businesses they view as a nuisance.

Remember to consider your family situation. How will you deal with child care, chores, time with your spouse, friends, etc.?

Whether or not you decide to base your business in your home also depends on the local zoning restrictions in your community (discussed further in chapter 11 on legal requirements) and the rental agreement you have with your landlord if you do not own your place of residence.

Consider your company image. There has been a growth in the number of home-based businesses in the last ten years, and the idea has become much more widely accepted. However, some people will not take seriously a business operating out of the home and it is important to follow a few guidelines that will make your home-based business look more professional.

For instance, install a separate telephone line and do not let children or other family members answer that line. If you are unable to take a call, use the answering machine or a voice messaging service. Use a post office box number as your business address if your home address is obviously a residential area or an apartment building.

If you anticipate having clients visit your home office, make sure you have a designated space, close to the entrance, that is only for business and decorated accordingly. If you do not have that type of space available, it would be wise not to invite clients to your home. Meet them outside of your home office.

The primary advantage to running a business out of your home is the small capital outlay necessary to get started. Having a lower overhead should free up money that you can use to invest in inventory and to promote and market your business.

Converting a spare bedroom or den on the ground floor of your home would be the ideal situation. A basement or attic is not as preferable because of accessibility problems and stairs. You will need an area to physically make the baskets, an office area, and a storage area. In order to have all three of these components in the same space, you would need approximately 400 square feet of space. If you do not have that much space to designate to your business, consider having your inventory and supplies storage in the garage or basement and your office in another area of the house.

The business of making gift packages and baskets can create a lot of mess, and you should have a work area that can be kept out of sight. Generally your customers will never see your work space, so it is unnecessary to invest in expensive furniture and decor. Use your capital to market your business.

There are numerous tax advantages to having your business in the home. To take full advantage of these tax breaks, your home-based operation must take up an entire room, which is devoted solely for the purpose of your business. These tax advantages are discussed in further detail in chapter 12 on accounting and taxes.

2. The business and your family

Most often the spouse who chooses to work at home is the one with primary responsibility for child care. Blending the two tasks is no easy matter, particularly with very young children. The needs of the children and the demands of the business are often at odds with each other.

Doing some advance thinking and preparing for it will help you deal with the conflict. Understand from the beginning that simply working at home may not completely eliminate child care concerns — although at first, when the demands of the business are small and you can easily adjust your schedule to conform to that of the children, it may seem so. This could change rapidly. It is best to think about how you will handle child care well in advance of starting your business. If your children are very young, you might consider these options:

(a) Work around your children's schedules

(b) Work while your children are in school

(c) Hire in-home care

(d) Take your children to out-of-home care

Your need for child care while running your business will depend on several factors, notably your financial objectives, the time required to meet those objectives, and the ages of your children. The children, however, regardless of age, will be affected by your decision to start your business from the home. Tell your children as openly as you can about your plans. Younger children need to understand, for example, that your gift basket supplies are not available for their art work.

Older children can understand the importance of your work and help out by assuming more household duties.

And while it is crucial to explain to family members the importance of your work, it is equally crucial that you balance the time between your work and family. It is sometimes difficult to leave a home-based business behind. Many home-based business operators find themselves going back to work after dinner, late at night, or on weekends.

For your sake and that of your family, don't turn yourself into a home workaholic. This is another reason for that separate, self-contained work space. Closing that door at the end of your work time gives you a clear dividing line between work and family needs.

Chapter 3
BUSINESS RESOURCES AND EQUIPMENT

As has been mentioned earlier, you need very little equipment to start up a gift basket business — but you do need some basic office equipment and services in place. This chapter discusses how to establish the basics for your business and provides options to consider so you can control your expenses. With a thorough review and comparison of the costs of the main overhead areas, you should require minimal capital investment and keep your overhead and risk to a minimum.

a. Business Resources

1. Mail services

If your office space is in your home, or if the space you lease or rent doesn't have an office image, rent a post office box from a private mailbox rental facility that offers a street address and suite number. This will allow you to have a suite number on your address and will present a more professional image. Most communities and neighborhoods have private postal outlets and you will find them convenient for a number of reasons.

The private mailing company I use for some of my out-of-town shipping offers all of the following services:

- 24-hour mailbox service with street address and suite number

- Mail receiving/forwarding

- Stamps and metered mail

- Packing, shipping, and supplies

- All forms of shipping — overnight, second day air, ground

- Fax service

- Photocopies

- Money transfer

- Money orders

- Telephone messaging/voice mail

- Business cards and stationery

- Office/shipping supplies

Having this type of business close by can be very advantageous, especially in the start-up phase of your company. Look in the Yellow Pages under Mail Boxes, Postal Box Rentals, or Postal Services to find a facility in your area.

2. *Business telephone line and fax line*

A business telephone line is more expensive than a regular personal line, but it is necessary if you want to be listed in the Yellow Pages and in the white pages under your company name. When you subscribe, be prepared to show your business license and/or incorporation documents. Depending on your credit rating, you may also be required to pay a refundable deposit.

For a new gift basket business, a single telephone line and a designated fax line should be sufficient. I highly recommend having a separate line and number for your fax machine. A great deal of your business will be conducted by fax, which is less time consuming than taking orders over the phone and much less expensive than long distance telephone calls.

It is to your advantage not to have your telephone line tied up by the fax machine, and there are many business fax machines that cannot connect to other fax machines that are tied into a phone line or answering machine. As your business grows, you may want to invest in a multi-line phone system which allows you to have two or more calls coming in or going out simultaneously. The hook-up fees and monthly charges for this type of service are expensive, and you should wait and see if the number of business calls you are receiving warrant the costs.

If you are purchasing new phones for your business, it may be wise to purchase multi-line phones as the cost between single line phones and multi-lines is nominal. Arrange a meeting with your local phone company sales representative. He or she will be able to explain in detail the services and options available to you.

3. Telephone options

When you choose your telephone system, remember that it is an essential piece of business equipment. The important consideration is the impression your telephone system gives your clients or prospective clients and how effectively you receive incoming messages.

The telephone business is highly competitive, and there are many options to choose from. Explore them all, and then choose those that suit both your budget and business needs.

(a) Call forwarding

This service allows you to forward your business telephone number to another location. This is an excellent option if you operate your business office in one location and your basket making facility in another.

(b) Call alert/call waiting

In the early stages of your business this is an inexpensive alternative to having a multi-line telephone. This service allows you to put one call on hold while you receive another.

(c) Programmable memory

This option on your telephone allows you to program frequently dialed numbers into the unit and can be a great time saver. It is also a good idea to program police and other emergency numbers.

(d) Speaker phone/hands-free

This option can be beneficial if you are put on hold frequently; it allows you to do other work while waiting for the person to pick up. Personally, I suggest taking the phone off hands-free when you are finally connected, as the quality of most speaker phones is poor and some clients dislike being put on speaker phones, but it might be a handy option if a call comes in when your hands are literally tied up making a basket.

(e) Cordless phone

This type of phone allows you to move freely around your office and eliminates the need to put someone on hold while you try to find a file across the room or look up information.

(f) Cellular phone

Cellular phones are expensive and most people do not give the number out to clients because you pay for incoming calls as well as outgoing. These phones can come in handy if you are out of the office frequently. You can also call forward your business number to a cellular phone, which is convenient if you are waiting for an important call. But generally, cell phones are too cost prohibitive to use as your regular business phone equipment.

(g) Voice messaging service

For a nominal monthly fee, you can hook into a messaging service provided by your phone company. I feel this is a much better alternative than using an answering machine to pick up messages. It comes across as being more professional and you can pick up messages and change your message from any location.

(h) Long-distance carriers

Since the deregulation of the telephone companies, there are numerous options available to the business owner for long-distance billing. These services vary from one area to the next, so your best option is to do your research well and talk to other small-to-medium-size business owners in your community to discover the best option for you. I recently made a switch from my local phone company to a new long-distance carrier and have decreased my long distance charges by approximately 40%.

(i) Toll-free phone and fax

As your business grows you will be surprised by how many customers you will have outside your local calling area. Because of the proliferation of toll-free numbers, many consumers are unwilling to pay for long distance charges when purchasing products from out-of-town companies. Many consumers will seek out companies that offer toll-free service. The cost of subscribing to a toll-free number has become very affordable and is an option that a small business should definitely consider.

The base monthly fee for my toll-free phone number and toll-free fax number is only $8 per month, and I am happy to pay the charges incurred for usage because of the business that is generated by those calls. If you are concerned that your suppliers or other business associates will take advantage of your toll-free number, you have the option of printing those numbers only on materials sent directly to potential clients.

Also consider a toll-free fax number. I send out a fax-back order form to my out-of-town clients. Taking orders by fax saves time and is considerably cheaper than by phone. It is also extremely important to have orders in writing, as it eliminates any misunderstandings, and is necessary if the customer is paying by credit card.

b. Deliveries and Transportation

Decide how you will make local deliveries, send out-of-town deliveries, and pick up your inventory and supplies. I know a gift basket company owner who spends more time on the road delivering and picking up than she does in her place of business. This is a common mistake that many small business owners make. They think that by doing the deliveries and picking up stock themselves they are saving money.

If you are going to be successful, the most important place for you to be is in your office, taking and making phone calls, receiving faxes, sending out quotations, ordering product, marketing your business, and making your gift packages. Being available when the phone rings and reacting immediately to requests will make all the difference to your success or failure. I operate my business on the premise that there is always someone available to take a call or make a presentation in the showroom during regular business hours. Operating this way gives you a leg up over the competition; you can have an order complete and out the door before your competition even gets around to answering their phone messages. If you are a one-person operation, organize a system that allows you to spend the maximum amount of time in your place of business.

1. Courier companies

Shop around for the right courier company for your business. Compare rates and meet with a couple of them before deciding on which company's services you will choose. A reliable courier service with friendly staff is vital to your company.

I use a courier company to deliver small packages and small orders of gift baskets. If you use one courier company exclusively and in volume, you should be able to negotiate a better rate. I charge my customers the same rate as I pay the courier company. Marking up courier charges is foolish, as many consumers are aware of what the charge should be.

2. Freight forwarding companies

There are many companies to choose from in this area, and again you should do some research and meet with several sales representatives to find the company that is right for your business. If you are going to use one company exclusively, and you have sufficient volume, you should be able to negotiate a better rate.

I use a company that picks up on a daily basis, delivers worldwide, has several different service options (overnight air, second-day air, Saturday delivery, ground service, etc.), invoices me on a monthly basis, has an automated tracking service, and provides a fully automated phone-in pick-up service. I also use this company to deliver all my inventory and supplies, which means I get a better rate on deliveries and I can count on the stock being delivered to my place of business on a daily basis.

3. Local delivery companies

Use this type of company to deliver large orders locally that a courier company would not be able to handle. Generally these are the same companies that move furniture and offices and would be used when you have very large volume orders. For example, if you have an order for 200 gift packages to be delivered to one location locally, the charge from this type of company would be approximately $50 or 25¢ per gift package. You can either work that fee into the total cost of the basket or charge your client separately for delivery. Again, it is false economy to try and save $50 by making ten trips in your own vehicle to make the delivery.

4. Company vehicle

Obviously, there are times when it will make good sense to use your own vehicle for company business. Any charges incurred while using your own vehicle for company business can be used as tax deductions. (See chapter 12 for more on record keeping and taxes.)

Spend as much time in your place of business as possible by trying to schedule any of these types of deliveries or pick ups early or late in the day or for a four-hour period one day of the week when you might arrange to pay someone to cover your telephones and office.

c. Basket-Making Equipment

There is actually very little equipment needed in starting up a gift basket company. The most essential item that you will need to get started is a worktable. Any type of three foot by eight foot table will be sufficient. However, for optimum comfort and tidiness you may want to have a custom worktable built. I was fortunate to find a table that was designed for storing and laying out architectural plans. It is the ideal worktable for making gift baskets.

The best worktable is higher than a normal table by one foot because you will be standing up to make your gift baskets. Having a table at least three feet high will eliminate much of the physical stress on your body that can occur when standing for long periods of time making up baskets.

Also ideal is having shelving built under the table to hold your supplies. Another option is having your worktable put on casters so it can be easily moved or rolled out of sight.

In addition to a worktable, you will need the following supplies:

- A pair of good, sharp scissors
- Cellophane tape and dispenser
- Cellophane wrap
- Staplers
- Hole punch
- A variety of baskets and containers
- Basket stuffing material

- Ribbon or raffia

- Gift tags

- Stickers

- Gift basket inventory (i.e., the products you put in the basket)

Your gift basket inventory can be freestanding, stored on wall shelving, or you can hang your baskets and containers from the ceiling or from large hooks on the wall. The key to being organized is having as much of the floor space as free as possible for making large basket orders.

The types of items you want to include in your gift basket inventory and managing that inventory is discussed in more detail in chapters 5 and 6.

d. Office Equipment

To set up an efficient office you will need some basic equipment. Keep in mind that it pays to shop around for these items and you may want to consider buying some used equipment. You should be able to purchase adequate equipment to get you started for approximately $500. Look for the following items:

(a) Desk: having an L-shaped desk with space for your computer and printer would be advantageous.

(b) Chair: purchase a good quality office chair on casters — your back will thank you for it.

(c) Filing cabinets: one for customer files and company documents and one for product information.

(d) Bookcase: or shelving for storing large catalogues, stationery, etc.

(e) Telephone: as discussed previously, you may want to purchase a telephone with multi-line capabilities so that you do not have to invest in new equipment when the time comes to add extra telephone lines. Depending on the options that you choose, expect to pay from $30 to $100 for a business telephone.

e. Electronic Equipment

A computer (with a modem), printer, and fax machine are essential for your business, allow you to present a professional image, and enable you to communicate quickly and efficiently with your prospective clients. However, you can easily become overwhelmed trying to make your decisions when shopping for these items. The technology for electronic equipment seems to be changing and improving daily.

Visit reputable dealers who offer training, will make service calls, and offer a phone-in help line. Do extensive research before committing to a system and make sure that the system is right for you and your type of operation.

1. Computer and printer

With the right computer and software, you will be able to efficiently do your bookkeeping and accounting, invoicing, payables, receivables, payroll, customer data base, and direct mail, and generate professional quotes and correspondence. If your computer has Internet capabilities, you can also set up your own Web site and process orders via e-mail (see chapter 8).

Prices for computer equipment vary from one area to the next and from one supplier to another. Purchasing this equipment can be a big investment, so keep in mind that prices change quickly — as does technology. Read some books and do your homework, shop around and compare prices, choose one supplier to purchase all your equipment, and don't be afraid to ask for a discount. You may also want to look into the option of leasing the equipment and paying for it over time.

2. Facsimile machine

For a gift basket business, fax machines offer an efficient and economical way to communicate to clients, suppliers, and business associates. Taking orders by fax allows you to have the order in writing and signed by the customer. A fax machine also enables you to place orders for merchandise in writing and to receive firm quotes in writing from your suppliers.

A fax machine is less expensive than an elaborate telephone system, eliminates time spent on the telephone which ties up your line, and eliminates any verbal misunderstandings.

Your fax machine can also serve as a photocopier in some cases, saving you the cost of buying a photocopier or paying a copying service.

If you have a computer with a modem, you can purchase software that will enable you to use your computer as a fax machine. If you decide on the fax-modem option, remember that while you can receive any kind of fax, you can only send information that is already on your computer. If you want to fax a brochure to a client, you will have to scan it into your computer before you can fax it using a fax-modem.

3. Answering machine

You will also need an answering machine if you do not use the voice messaging option discussed earlier in this chapter. Many people feel answering machines are not personal enough and prefer a telephone answering service. They are willing to pay more for the personal touch.

As telephone answering machines grow in use, they are increasingly acceptable. Whatever your personal preference, do not leave a business line unanswered. Your recorded voice on a machine is much less damaging to your business than a phone that rings and rings.

If you do get an answering machine, make certain that the recorded message is courteous, short, and professional. If the message is too long, chances are the person calling will not stay on the line long enough to leave a message.

You can now get inexpensive answering machines that allow you to record more than one message and pick up your messages from remote locations, which is useful if you have to be out of the office for a few hours.

4. Other

I don't think a small gift basket company should invest in a photocopy machine. You can make file copies of correspondence on your computer printer and any other copying needs can be done at your printer. Some fax machines are able to photocopy, and there are growing numbers of inexpensive, 24-hour photocopying outlets.

f. Office Supplies

1. Custom printing

Your graphic designer should provide you with camera-ready black and white artwork (or computer files) for each of the following components. The price you pay for these items will depend on the paper stock you choose and the numbers of colors to be printed. Following is a general example of what you can expect to pay for custom stationery on good quality paper stock printed with one color:

- 500 — 2″ x 3″ business cards: $65
- 2,000 — 8″ x 11″ letterhead: $154
- 1,000 — #10 business-size envelopes: $85
- 1,000 — 2″ x 3″ folded gift tags: $75
- 1,000 — 3″ x 2″ company information insert card: $65
- 2,000 — 2″ x 2″ high gloss stick-on labels: $295

How to use your business stationery to your advantage in your advertising and marketing plan is discussed in more detail in chapter 8.

2. General office supplies

To get started you will need to invest in some general office supplies. I have found that the best prices will be found at large warehouse-type retailers, such as Office Depot, Costco, and Price Club. Following is a list of the office supplies you will need to start your business:

- Pens and pencils
- Markers
- Post-it notes
- Pads of paper
- Paper clips
- Large, year-at-a-glance wall calendar
- Cash receipt book
- File folders
- Large mailing envelopes

- Cellophane tape

- Packing tape

- Scissors

- Three-hole punch

- Binders

- Computer and fax machine supplies: paper, printing cartridge, etc.

- Miscellaneous desk accessories

Plan on budgeting $200 to $300 for start-up office supplies. See Sample 1 for an example of what your initial estimates and start-up cost analysis might look like. See the next chapter for information on overall start-up costs.

SAMPLE 1
BUSINESS START-UP COST

Purchases for:	Studio/Office	Home-based
Office furniture	$500	$500
Telephone	150	150
Answering machine	75	75
Computer and printer	3,500	3,500
Computer software	500	500
Fax machine	600	600
Basket making equipment	200	200
Basket preparation table	100	100
Storage shelves	200	200
Graphic design services	1,000	500
Photography	1,000	0
Brochures*	3,000	1,000
Initial stationery and business cards	750	250
Initial opening inventory	2,500	1,500
Office supplies	300	300
Legal	800	800
Accounting set-up	500	500
Rent security deposit	500	0
TOTAL	**$16,175**	**$10,675**

Home-based is estimated on $65,000 in sales
Studio/office space is based on $250,000 in sales.

* Brochure costs based on
   2,000 three-panel, 8" x 11" brochures
    Studio: four-color
    Home-based: two-color

Chapter 4

YOUR FINANCIAL INVESTMENT AND PLAN

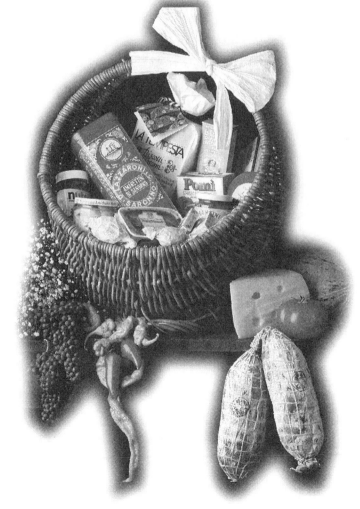

a. Financing Your Venture

Starting a business takes capital, and even if your envisioned gift basket company is home-based and operating on a seasonal basis, you will need to have enough money to get started and keep going until the orders and cash start to flow. The financing for your venture may come from a variety of sources: personal savings, family and friends, financial institutions, business partners, and private investors.

Most business funding comes from a combination of the above. Before you think about borrowing money, keep in mind the risks involved. As a small business owner, you should always feel a little bit uneasy about debt and work hard to keep it under control. If it is necessary to borrow money, borrow only what you need and only when you need it. Following are several options for financing your business venture.

1. Personal savings

The ideal situation for starting a new business is financing it yourself. If you have the personal resources to run your business until it returns a profit, you will have no lenders to account to, no bank interest to pay, and no financial responsibilities other than to yourself and your company. There is no better or less stressful way to start a new enterprise than debt free.

If the financial demands of your new business are small, you may want to consider waiting until you have the savings to independently finance your venture. If you are starting a larger venture that needs more initial capital, it will still be necessary to show potential lenders and investors that you have something more to invest than just your ideas and time.

2. Family and friends

Many small business ventures start with the generosity of family and friends. Most often this type of financing takes the form of a loan on trust, accepted in good faith, with no collateral required. There is always a danger in mixing business financing with personal relationships and it should be approached with careful consideration; the terms and conditions of the loan should be reasonable and negotiated in a businesslike manner. Have a lawyer prepare a legal promissory note that outlines all the terms and conditions.

Most important, be certain you will have the ability to pay the money back on time and in full. Before accepting the loan, think about a backup payment plan should the business be unable to repay the debt.

3. Banks

The most logical approach to securing a loan from a financial institution is to select one where you already have a history of responsible financial dealings and an already established relationship with the manager or loans officer.

Be well prepared when you approach any potential lender. Have a clear, concise, typed, well-presented business plan. Present the lender with your sales and cash flow projections, and explain precisely how much money you want to borrow and why. Be very specific and show how your business can be expected to generate the cash to repay the loan.

Be prepared to show statements of your personal net worth and what other financial resources you have available to start up your business. If you want to win the confidence of the bank manager or loans officer, be prepared to answer all questions truthfully and candidly.

It is unlikely that you will be able to secure a bank loan unless you have some tangible assets as security. If you own a home and are willing to mortgage it, or mortgage it further, a lender is more likely to let you borrow.

When you borrow money for your new business, you are personally liable to pay it back. Even if your company is incorporated, the lender will require a personal guarantee from you. If they agree to grant you a loan, financial institutions will usually require you to take out property and liability insurance on your business and a life insurance policy on yourself, naming the bank as beneficiary.

A financial institution may come up with a variety of reasons for turning down your request for a loan. If you do not succeed at the first lender you try, go to others. Ask why you are being turned down for financing and make adjustments accordingly. Perhaps you need to revamp your business plan or start your business on a smaller scale. You may also want to consider taking out a personal loan, which is sometimes the easiest method for many small business entrepreneurs to secure financing, especially when the amount needed for start up is small. You will still need to have collateral and satisfy the bank of your ability to pay, but it is not necessary to provide the bank with a business plan or go into the details of your proposed venture.

4. Private investors

Going into business with someone you know can be difficult — with someone you don't know it can be impossible and usually comes with stringent conditions. The best source for finding private investors is your accountant. People with money to invest in small start-up ventures often rely on their accountants for advice.

Expect such investors to be cautious and to attach conditions to the loan. Their approach to lending money to a small business is similar to that of a bank, and you will need to provide them with all the same type of information that you would when applying for a loan with any financial institution. Private investors will seldom invest in a small business venture unless there is a possibility of a greater than average return on investment.

5. Government

The governments of both the United States and Canada provide financial assistance to small business.

In the United States, the Small Business Administration (SBA) exists to help small business educationally and financially. You should check your phone book for the office nearest you and see a counselor for current information on funding. You can also call the SBA's Small Business Answer Desk at 1-800-827-5722.

Remember, the SBA is a government agency and the winds of politics often cause shifts in its direction. Make sure your information is firsthand before you apply for funds.

In Canada, money for small business comes from a variety of government departments both provincial and federal. Check the small business development department of your provincial government.

It should be noted that most government lending is done as "last resort" lending. It often takes the form of loan guarantees rather than direct loans. You may have to prove you were unable to obtain money from other sources. Generally, they will expect that you have some of your own money invested in the enterprise. There may also be restrictions on the type of businesses that receive funding. Learn what is available through the various levels of government.

Before approaching any government lending department for funds, prepare proper documentation on your business. The rules of preparation and professionalism apply any time you seek either commercial or government financial assistance.

Many government programs give loans or loan guarantees to incorporated businesses only. Small proprietorships often find themselves ineligible for certain types of government funding. Even if you do strike out, the process of learning what is available is worthwhile. You may not be eligible now, but there may be a time later in your business cycle when your business will qualify, and the time spent will not have been wasted.

b. *Your Business Plan*

A good business plan is a simple, honest document that completely and precisely describes your experience, your proposed business, and your long-term plans for that business. It does not need to be long or complicated; it should tell a complete story that can be easily understood by a potential lender or investor.

A business plan is expected to follow a standard format, but it should be tailored to suit the situation. How your business plan is presented is as important as the information it contains.

It should be prepared on a typewriter or word processor, double-spaced on white standard-size paper. Have someone else proofread it and make sure that there are no mistakes or spelling and grammatical errors.

It should have a separate cover page with the company name, address, telephone and fax numbers, and your name as the person to contact for further information. It should also show the date that the document was prepared. Each section of the plan should have a heading and the pages should be numbered.

You may want to consider writing a short covering letter offering to provide any additional information that might be required. If you write a covering letter, make sure the person's name and title to whom you are writing are correct.

A business plan that includes three or four pages of solid information and a cash flow forecast will probably be sufficient for starting up a small gift basket company. If you have done thorough market research and financial forecasts you will have all the information necessary to write a business plan.

Following is a brief discussion of each of the components you will need to generate your plan.

1. Executive summary

Outline the following essential facts of your proposed business:

    (a) Type of business

    (b) Location of the business

    (c) Legal structure of the business (proprietorship, partnership, incorporated company)

    (d) Names of any other shareholders

    (e) The amount of funds required

    (f) The terms under which those funds will be repaid

2. Personal experience and background

This section includes your up-to-date resume and those of any partners or other key people in your proposed venture. Emphasize why your background and experience or that of your partner or key personnel is valuable to the success of your business. It is critical that potential lenders or investors feel that you have the experience and expertise to make your business work. They are very aware that mismanagement can be a cause of business failure.

3. Description of product and service

Describe your gift basket products and service clearly and concisely. Explain why there is a need for your service and why it will do well in your chosen market. Emphasize the advantages your products have over those of your competition. Make sure you highlight your product's uniqueness. Emphasize that your business will be home-based or in low-cost studio space with low overhead, which will allow you to sell your product at a reasonable price.

4. Sales and marketing strategy

Prove that you have done your market research and provide details on who your customers are and how you intend to reach them. Explain how you will use the information that you have gathered as the basis of your sales and marketing strategy. Describe your competition and why your products will sell in your targeted market. Show that you have a good understanding of your chosen market and why a potential lender should feel confident that your sales and marketing planning will be successful.

5. Forecasts and projections

This section of your business plan should be a summary of everything discussed in the next chapter, which includes your cost of sales analysis, fixed expenses and overhead, planned sales and marketing expenses, start-up costs, projected sales forecast, and a projected cash flow analysis. Your cash flow forecast should be a truthful and realistic projection of the sales and cash needs of your new business. It should show the potential lender that the business has the ability to pay back the amount borrowed. This is generally where most lenders will be looking for ways to shoot holes in your plan, so be prepared for scrutiny and to answer any questions regarding your proposed business.

For more detailed advice on business plans, consult *Preparing a Successful Business Plan*, another title in the Self-Counsel Business Series.

Chapter 5
FINANCIAL MANAGEMENT

Careful financial planning is crucial when establishing a new business venture, not only in the start-up stage as discussed in the last chapter, but continually once your business is established. Planning or forecasting your sales and expenses may seem like an impossible challenge for the new business owner because there is no financial history to base your forecast on, but it can and must be done. You need to have two simple issues in mind as you start your new venture: what the costs are and what sales you can expect from your business. Following are some reasons for forecasting sales and expenses for your new venture:

(a) To give you a good indication of the funds required for start-up

(b) To prove or disprove the feasibility of your idea

(c) To encourage you to think practically about the factors critical to your business such as costs, space requirements, equipment purchases, etc.

(d) To allow you to see your business on paper before you invest any money

(e) To indicate at what point your venture will break even and begin to show a profit

(f) To help a lender or investor see the merits and potential profitability of your business

(g) To prepare you for the possible risks of starting a business and guide you in your personal financial planning

(h) To tell you how long your start-up capital will last and at what point you will need to rely on the cash flow from sales to operate the business

In order to do a financial forecast, you must know and be able to predict the following:

(a) What is the amount of cash on hand you have to invest in your new business?

(b) What amount of loans or borrowed money from outside sources is available?

(c) What is your business capacity? How many gift baskets can you realistically produce?

(d) What will you charge for your product?

(e) What does it cost to produce your product?

(f) Based on your sales and marketing efforts, how many gift baskets can you sell?

(g) What are the fixed expenses of running your business?

a. Forecasting Cash Flow

The most important forecast for a new business is cash flow. Your accounts receivable and your accounts payable are estimated and allocated to the month that they occur. Creating a cash flow forecast gives you a picture of cash movement through the business, both coming in and going out. Having a clear picture of your business cash flow will help you plan major purchases and expenditures. You will not make the mistake of producing an expensive new color brochure or taking a large bonus if you know that your cash is going out rather than coming in.

Understanding cash flow is an absolute necessity for the new business owner. Along with loans and your personal investment, the cash flow into your business is created by the sales of your gift baskets. The amount of cash your business will earn will depend on the number of baskets that you sell and the price you charge.

In chapter 6, we discuss setting a price for your baskets, based on a full mark-up or a 50% gross profit margin, which is the most common mark-up for a gift basket company in an office or studio space or a home-based operation. The cash flow out of your business is the result of the costs of producing your gift baskets and the expenses of running your business. Your objective should be to bring in more cash than goes out. To plan and monitor that process you need to develop a cash flow forecast.

b. Cost of Sales and Inventory

Each different gift package that you decide to produce should go through a cost analysis. If you have decided to sell and market eight different gift packages, then you need to do a worksheet for each one and then multiply that number by the amount of baskets you will have as stock on hand, or as your opening inventory. For example:

Basket: "Gourmet Treasures"

Basket or container — $4.00
Mineral water — $1.25
Brie cheese — $2.60
Pâté — $3.00
Antipasto — $2.40
Water crackers — $1.30
Chocolates — $4.00
Pâté/cheese spreader — $0.50
Cocktail napkins — $0.50
Packaging — $1.45

Total cost — $21.00

Selling price — $42.00

Total opening inventory (based on having stock to make 12 baskets) = $21.00 x 12 = $252.00

If you decide to carry 8 different baskets ranging from a selling price of $20 to $75 each, or a cost of $10 to $37.50 each, and have stock on hand to produce up to 24 of the lower-cost baskets and up to 6 of the more expensive baskets, you would need approximately $1,500 to $2,000 for your opening inventory. This investment would include all your baskets and containers, food or gift products, basket stuffing, ribbons, and cellophane.

In the early stages of your venture, it is probably wise to keep the number of standard gift packages you carry between 8 and 12 and increase that number as you get a feel for your market and what type of gifts turn over the fastest. See the following chapter for more information on inventory and pricing.

c. Fixed Expenses and Overhead

Fixed expenses and overhead are the costs incurred in running your business and are constant regardless of how many baskets you produce or what your sales volume is. Make a list of all the expenses that will be paid by your company and whether they are monthly, quarterly, or annual expenses.

See Sample 2 for an example of overhead expenses that could be incurred by a gift basket company.

Worksheet 2 is for you to figure out your own expenses. When doing your own list, eliminate items that do not apply to your operation and add any that are missing.

d. Marketing Costs

In addition to your fixed costs and the cost of inventory, there are costs incurred in marketing your products and services. In order to do a cash flow you must have a marketing plan (see chapter 9 on sales and marketing) and forecast a budget for your first year of operation. Included in your marketing plan should be the expenses listed in Sample 3.

e. Start-Up Costs

Start-up costs include your purchases for all the equipment, furniture, and sales materials necessary to start your new venture. Worksheet 3 is a list of some of the start-up expenses that might be incurred by a new gift basket company. Eliminate those that do not apply to your operation and add any that are missing to work out your start-up expenses.

f. Forecasting Sales

Forecasting the sales for your first year of operation is one of the most difficult steps in preparing your cash flow projections and business plan. Review your market research materials and estimate how many customers you can hope to attract each month. Be realistic and take into consideration the seasonal impact of your business and how much you can produce. How many gift baskets can you produce in a day, a week, and a month?

SAMPLE 2
OVERHEAD AND FIXED EXPENSES

Studio/office:	Monthly	Quarterly	Annually
Advertising	$400	$2,200	$9,550
Rent	500	1,500	6,000
Telephone line	60	180	720
Fax line	60	180	720
Utilities	50	150	600
Automobile	100	300	1,200
Office supplies	50	150	600
Postage	50	150	600
Photocopies	20	60	240
Shipping	30	90	360
Courier charges	20	60	240
Dues and memberships	20	60	240
Travel	25	75	300
Licenses			100
Insurance	50	150	600
Accounting			1,000
Legal			150
Health plan	40	120	480
Equipment rental	10	30	120
Wages and benefits	1,000	3,000	12,000
Interest and bank charges	20	60	240
TOTAL	**$2,505**	**$8,515**	**$36,060**

Home-based:	Monthly	Quarterly	Annually
Advertising	$48	$144	$3,250
Telephone/fax	60	180	720
Utilities	33	100	400
Automobile	100	300	1,200
Office supplies	50	150	600
Postage	50	150	600
Photocopies	20	60	240
Shipping	15	45	180
Courier charges	10	30	120
Dues and memberships	20	60	240
Travel	25	75	300
Licenses			100
Insurance			500
Accounting		250	1,000
Legal			150
Interest and bank charge	20	60	240
TOTAL	**$451**	**$1,604**	**$9,840**

WORKSHEET 2
BUSINESS EXPENSES

Expense	$ Amount		
	Monthly	Quarterly	Annually
Advertising	_____	_____	_____
Rent	_____	_____	_____
Telephone line	_____	_____	_____
Fax line	_____	_____	_____
Yellow Pages listing	_____	_____	_____
Utilities	_____	_____	_____
Automobile	_____	_____	_____
Office supplies	_____	_____	_____
Postage	_____	_____	_____
Photocopies	_____	_____	_____
Shipping	_____	_____	_____
Courier charges	_____	_____	_____
Dues and memberships	_____	_____	_____
Travel	_____	_____	_____
Licenses	_____	_____	_____
Insurance	_____	_____	_____
Accounting	_____	_____	_____
Legal	_____	_____	_____
Health plan	_____	_____	_____
Equipment rental	_____	_____	_____
Wages and benefits	_____	_____	_____
Interest and bank charges	_____	_____	_____

SAMPLE 3
MARKETING EXPENSES

Item	$ Amount		
	Monthly	Quarterly	Annually
Print advertising	_____	_____	_____
Web advertising	_____	_____	_____
Yellow Pages	_____	_____	_____
Direct mail	_____	_____	_____
Trade shows	_____	_____	_____
Special events	_____	_____	_____
Promotions	_____	_____	_____
Others	_____	_____	_____
Others	_____	_____	_____
Others	_____	_____	_____
Others	_____	_____	_____
Others	_____	_____	_____

WORKSHEET 3
START-UP EXPENSES

Purchase	$ Amount
Office furniture	_____
Telephone	_____
Answering machine	_____
Computer and printer	_____
Computer software	
Fax machine	_____
Basket-making equipment	_____
Table	_____
Photography	_____
Storage shelves	_____
Graphic design services	_____
Brochure printing	_____
Initial supply stationery and business cards	_____
Initial opening inventory	_____

Also take into consideration the amount of time necessary to get your marketing and sales materials into circulation and to build a customer base. What is the average dollar amount of a gift basket sale? I personally use an average sale of $30 per basket, but it could be lower or higher depending on your market.

Prepare a chart by month of the sales that you think you can anticipate. Consider planned vacations, other personal commitments, seasonal influences, special promotions, time it takes to build sales, and when you can expect results from your advertising and marketing efforts. Do several different versions, the lowest being the amount of sales necessary each month to reach a break-even point after your fixed expenses. See Sample 4 for an outline of monthly sales forecasts.

At this point you should have all the information you need on the cost of sales and inventory, fixed expenses and overhead, start-up costs, and projected sales for one year. Now you are ready to prepare a forecast. You can do this manually using a 13-column accounting pad or on a computer if you have access to one with spreadsheet software.

Either way it is absolutely necessary for the ongoing success of your business to prepare these financial forecasts now and on an ongoing basis as your business grows and prospers. Good financial management helps you control your business and plan for success.

SAMPLE 4
MONTHLY SALES FORECAST

Month	Seasonal or Special Considerations	# Units Sold	$ Total
January	_____	_____	_____
February	_____	_____	_____
March	_____	_____	_____
April	_____	_____	_____
May	_____	_____	_____
June	_____	_____	_____
July	_____	_____	_____
August	_____	_____	_____
September	_____	_____	_____
October	_____	_____	_____
November	_____	_____	_____
December	_____	_____	_____

Chapter 6
PLANNING AND PRICING YOUR GIFT BASKETS

In your first year of operation, you should concentrate on selling gift baskets and gift packages only. As your customer base increases, you can think about expanding your business gradually into other gift merchandise areas such as local arts and crafts, souvenir tourist items, books, awards, speaker's gifts, paper goods, advertising specialty items (goods that have a corporate identity imprinted on them), etc. But keep things simple the first year until you can assess where increased markets are, how an expanding inventory will affect your costs, and if you can — or want to — manage a large range of products.

a. Your Gift Basket Designs

1. Establish some standard designs

Decide on the number of different gift packages that you want to offer on a year-round basis. These will be the items that you will keep an inventory of and always have on hand to produce quickly. Six to 12 different gift package designs would be standard for most companies starting out. This is where your own imagination and creativity will come into play.

Following are some gift packaging ideas for various occasions and different price points:

- **New baby: "Welcome to the World"**
  Container: Doll-size wicker chair painted white
  Ingredients: Stuffed toy appropriate for either a girl or boy, specialty baby shampoo and conditioner, parents' magazine, toiletry products for mom, chocolate truffles, decorative bottle of mineral water (split of champagne optional).

- **Gardener's gift: "The Avid Gardener"**
  Container: Large, terra-cotta pot
  Ingredients: Seeds, gardening gloves, gardening tools, gardener's hand soap, wildflower calendar, gardening book.

- **Gourmet's gift: "That's Italian"**
  Container: Enamel colander
  Ingredients: Gourmet dried pasta, sun-dried tomatoes, antipasto, pesto, oregano, olive oil, cookbook.

- **"House Warming"**
  Container: Painted wood toolbox
  Ingredients: Hammer, picture hooks, flashlight, night light, live plant, split of champagne with two glasses.

- **"Some Like it Hot"**
  Container: Fire engine-red metal bucket
  Ingredients: Bloody Mary mix, salsa, Tabasco, spicy snack mix, five-alarm chili spices, hot crackers, spicy antipasto.

- **"Anti-Stress Survival Kit"**
  Container: Decorative hat box
  Ingredients: Candles, bubble bath, bath oil, aroma therapy products, chocolate truffles, split of champagne.

- **"Coffee Break"**
  Container: Decorative coffee mug
  Ingredients: Old-fashioned cocoa mix, shortbread, energy snack, chocolate truffle bar.

- **"Bon Voyage — First Mate"**
  Container: Authentic captain's hat
  Ingredients: Toy ship and rubber duck, plush toy, games, cookies, snacks, and chocolates.

- **"Home on the Range"**
  Container: Straw cowboy hat
  Ingredients: Natural wood excelsior basket stuffing, bandana, book of cowboy quotations, mini-souvenir branding iron, salsa, chips, chili spices, pepper jelly, spicy peanuts. Tie the package with natural raffia and rope and a bolo tie.

- **"Way Down South"**
  Container: Small cast iron skillet
  Ingredients: Jambalaya mix, filé powder, red beans and rice, Tabasco sauce, Cajun cookbook, tape of Cajun cooking music. Tie the package with purple, gold, and green Mardi Gras beads and ribbons.

- **"East Coast Basket"**
  Container: Lobster trap
  Ingredients: Plush lobster toy, cookbook, chowder mix, bisque mix, lobster pâté, and other regional food items.

- **"New Job"**
  Container: Heavy cardboard file box covered with decorative paper
  Ingredients: Pencils, pencil sharpener, pen, imprinted Post-it notes, small sewing kit, mini-office first aid kit, special coffee mug, gourmet coffee, energy bars, and a container filled with wrapped mints.

- **"First Day of Spring" or "Earth Day"**
  Container: Metal watering can
  Ingredients: Live tree seedling or tree-growing seeds, gardening hand soap, gardener's lip balm, gardener's bath soak, gardening book, gardening gloves, and natural energy bars.

As you can see, all of the above gift packages are in useful containers that show a little bit of imagination. The possibilities are endless and you will be surprised by the number of containers you can come up with when you start to think about it. The more innovative you can be with your products, the better you will stand apart from your competition.

2. Custom-made baskets

When suggesting gift basket ideas to your clients it is essential to be creative and to come up with ideas that they would never have thought of themselves. That is what will set you apart from your competition and will build loyal repeat customers. I cannot stress enough that you must get as much information as possible from your client about the recipient. A well-received retirement basket or birthday basket will depend on how much you know about the person who is going to receive it. Once you have ascertained what the lifestyle and interests of the recipient are, you will be able to design a custom basket or gift that will be just right.

As an exercise, make a list of all the unique containers you can think of and then make a list of packages that you could include in those containers. Be sure to think about what type of basket stuffing or embellishments you would use and what type of materials you would use to tie the package.

Following are a few ideas to get you started in making up your own basket idea list.

(a) Secretary's Day

Secretary's Day has become a strong gift basket giving occasion and is an excellent opportunity for executives and employers to show appreciation for the support staff who help their organizations run smoothly. Design baskets with a gold theme or a star theme as "you are worth your weight in gold" or "you are the star." Use a metallic gold container, basket, or painted bowl as the base, gold Mylar tissue and basket fill, gold star embellishments, gold moir, napkins, cellophane printed with gold stars, and a gold bow. Inside the basket you might include a gold coffee mug, gold pen or pencil, celestial design vase or notepaper, small gold-wrapped candy, gourmet coffee, and chocolate truffle bar.

(b) Valentine picnic basket

Use a heart-shaped basket with red basket fill and add a picnic cloth, two matching napkins, and champagne flutes. Fill the basket with a heart-shaped box of chocolates, fresh fruit, crackers, Brie cheese, smoked oysters, pâté, champagne, candles, and relaxing bath crystals. Tie the package with fancy lace ribbons.

(c) Bon voyage/stateroom party

A large decorative cruise ship gift box filled with mineral water, salmon pâté, antipasto, Brie cheese, water crackers, cookies, chocolates, toffee popcorn, hot drink mix, biscotti, paper napkins, and cheese spreader. Tie the package with bon voyage ribbons and include a package of bon voyage streamers.

b. Keep Basic Items in Stock

Stock three sizes of gourmet food baskets that can be offered at various price points and for any number of occasions. Many basket wholesalers sell baskets in sets of three, and to get the best price, it is necessary to purchase them that way.

Following is a list of food items that would be standard for a gift basket company to carry. You should always have a basic stock of these products on hand and keep an inventory list of the products and their prices next to the telephone as customers will inevitably want you to make substitutions of products from your standard baskets.

- Decorative glass bottle of mineral water
- Crackers or water biscuits
- Pâté — shrimp, salmon, crab, venison, liver, etc.
- Smoked oysters
- Cheeses
- Snacks — nuts, trail mix, gourmet popcorn, bagel chips
- Cookies and shortbread
- Chocolate bars
- Boxes of chocolate
- Jams and preserves
- Honey
- Chutney and condiments
- Teas, coffees, cocoa mixes
- Dried pastas and spices
- Regional specialties from your area
- Standard gift items (mugs, glasses, pots, bowls, toys, etc.)

All of the products that you stock should be nonperishable and should have a shelf-life of 12 months or more. Not only should all of the products you carry taste wonderful, but the packaging must be special as well. You are not looking for items that would be found on the supermarket shelves, but in more exclusive gourmet food shops.

To source these products you will need to contact wholesale food suppliers in your area and ask them to send you a product list and have a sales rep come pay you a visit.

It is also possible to find smaller gourmet food producers at regional gift shows in your area. **Note:** Make sure that the suppliers of all your food products are licensed to be wholesale manufacturers. I once purchased some wonderful mango chutney from a small supplier only to have the lids blow off in my storage room. I was lucky that this happened before I ever used the product in gift packages; it would have been very embarrassing, or worse, I could have poisoned someone (see section **d.** in chapter 11 on liability insurance).

c. Buy Packaging Inventory

In addition to the containers, baskets, gift items, and food products, you will need to buy packaging inventory. These items are the decorative items used to package your gift baskets, which make them special and set you apart from the competition. Gift packaging inventory will include the following items.

1. Basket or container stuffing

Your basket stuffing can be in the form of shredded tissue, dyed wood shavings, shredded Mylar, or shredded colored cellophane. All of these materials come in a wide variety of colors and prices. You will need to stock several different types, depending on the style of basket you are selling. For example, it would probably be inappropriate to put shiny Mylar stuffing in a country-style gardener's basket.

2. Cellophane wrap

Cellophane wrap comes in rolls of various lengths and is also available in a variety of styles, such as clear, colored dots, solid colors, and with various patterns and prints. I always buy the biodegradable variety, and I publish that fact in my gift catalogue. You will want to have several sizes so that you can accommodate small to very large baskets and to enable you to choose the type most appropriate for the gift package.

3. Ribbon

There are hundreds of styles and colors of ribbon to choose from, and again what you buy will depend on the type of look you are trying to achieve and the type of gift package you are selling.

4. Raffia

Raffia, the fiber of the raffia palm used for tying and making baskets and hats, is now available in a wide range of colors and gives a more natural look to gift packages when used instead of ribbon.

5. Gift tags, gift cards, and gift labels

It is very important that your gift tags, cards, and labels all be custom designed for your company and include your phone number on them. I have made many new customers out of the satisfied recipients of one of my gift packages.

Following are the names and toll-free numbers for two major suppliers of gift packaging merchandise:

Gift Box Corporation of America
17 showrooms in the United States
1-800-GIFTBOX

Classic Packaging
Three locations in Canada
1-800-663-0881

d. Tips for Making Baskets

Once you have your inventory in front of you, you should practice making a few baskets to confirm how much inventory you need for each basket. Here are some basket-making tips:

(a) Most containers and baskets need to be filled with some type of paper fill before you use the more expensive basket stuffing, although this might not be necessary if your container is very shallow. Purchase a bale of clean newsprint or packing paper, which is inexpensive and is usually sold in 25 or 50 pound bales. Crumple the clean paper and fill the container almost to the top. Cover the paper with a solid piece of tissue paper that matches the basket stuffing you have chosen. Cover the tissue paper with a thin layer of basket stuffing. Make sure your colors are coordinated.

(b) Products should be standing up and angled into the basket or container. If the products sink down, you will need to add more packing material to raise their height.

(c) Place larger and heavier items in the back of the container.

(d) Place the most expensive item front and center. Labels should show so the recipients can see what they are getting.

(e) Fill empty spaces with small items, cookies, candies, and embellishments. Embellishments and enhancements increase the perceived value of the package.

(f) Measure your cellophane so that it covers the basket but doesn't leave too much on top after you have tied up the package.

(g) When filling large orders, use the assembly line method. After you have made up one sample basket, cut the cellophane and ribbon for the entire basket order. Place the empty baskets on your work space and fill all of them with the packing paper, tissue, and basket stuffing. Fill the baskets with all the products to be included. Add any embellishments at the time of wrapping the baskets in the cellophane. This method is faster and more efficient than trying to make one complete basket at a time.

(h) Learn to tie a few different types of decorative bows. Sample 5 shows how to tie two types of bows.

e. Sources of Inventory

Contact all the wholesale food suppliers listed in your local Yellow Pages and make appointments to visit their showrooms or have a sales representative visit you. When you have seen all the products and have the price lists, try to choose products that can be supplied by two or three of the companies. Most wholesale food suppliers have a minimum order and will often include delivery if the order is at a certain dollar amount. If there is one product from a supplier that you simply must have, be prepared to always buy it on a cash and carry basis because it is unlikely that the company will be willing to set up an account with you if you are ordering limited amounts of inventory.

POM-POM BOW

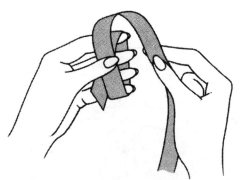

1 Roll the ribbon around your left-hand fingers.

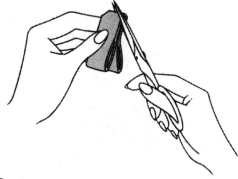

2 Fold the rolled up ribbon in the middle and cut off the two upper edges, diagonally.

3 Open up the fold and tie the narrow ribbon in the grooves.

4 Pull up the single loops from the inside by turning them left, then right, then to the middle.

5 Your bow is finished.

TULLE BOW

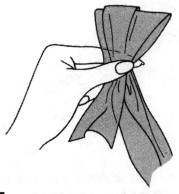

1 Fold the ribbon in a zigzag, one layer on top of the other.

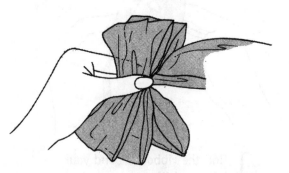

2 Layer four to eight times, depending on required size.

3 Fasten the loops with the small ribbon in the middle.

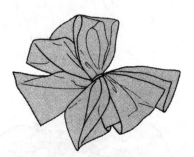

4 Spread out the single loops like a fan.

Attend regional gift shows. Gift shows are held twice a year all over North America usually in January/February and August/September (see the Appendix). There are two excellent publications that list all the gift shows world-wide and also publish a manufacturers directory once a year that can be most helpful in finding new products. I highly recommend subscribing to at least one of these publications:

Gifts & Decorative Accessories Magazine
Geyer-McAllister Publications Inc.
51 Madison Avenue
New York, New York
U.S.A. 10010

Gifts & Tablewares
1450 Don Mills Road
Don Mills, Ontario
Canada M3B 2X7

Almost every gift show will have demonstrations on how to make gift baskets, and many of the basket and packaging wholesalers will also have open houses twice a year where they will have gift basket-making seminars. Attending a seminar or demonstration will give you the opportunity to try out different materials and learn from experts in the business.

Gift shows are not open to the general public. When you register, be prepared to show a business license, business card, company check, copy of a paid invoice from a wholesale supplier, and personal identification. Once you have registered and your company is on file, you should not have to go through this process again. Always bring many business cards since suppliers will expect one before they will give out their wholesale price list.

f. Purchasing Inventory

After you have designed your gift packages, you need to place orders for your opening inventory. Type up a purchase order for the merchandise you want to buy and put quantities, individual prices, and a total on the purchase order. I usually fax my purchase orders to the supplier as it is faster than giving an order over the phone. When the goods are delivered, match the invoice or packing slip to the purchase order to determine that you have not been over or under shipped and that the price you have been charged is correct.

See Sample 6 for an example of a purchase order.

ENTERPRISES INC.

PURCHASE ORDER

April 7, 200-

To: **JEN MARKETING**   Fax: 555-9918

Re: Purchase order #0001

I would like to place an order for the following items:

   1 case of 48 smoked salmon pâté @ $96.00 per case

   2 cases of antipasto 125 ml size @ $24.00 per case of 12 = $48.00

   2 cases of plain water buscuits @ $24.00 per case of 24 = $48.00

   Total order = $192.00

We need to have this order in our office no later than Wednesday April 13th. Please let us know if there will be a problem with delivery. Thank you.

Kind Regards,
Foster-Walker Enterprises Inc.
Per:

Mardi Foster-Walker

201-1200 West Pender Street
Vancouver, B.C. Canada V6E 2S9
Phone: (toll free) 1-800-668-8813
Fax: (toll free) 1-800-668-6855
Phone: (604) 681-2456
Fax: (604) 681-2003

g. Inventory Control

Each supplier you make purchases from should be set up on an inventory control sheet. This sheet would have the following information:

   (a) Name, address, phone and fax number, and contact person at the supplier company

   (b) Stock number of the merchandise item

   (c) Case pack quantity

   (d) Cost price of the merchandise item

   (e) Opening inventory quantity

   (f) Reorder quantity

At my company, we take a physical inventory of all our gift basket stock every Monday morning and place orders on Monday afternoon so that we will have the goods before the following weekend. The frequency of taking inventory will be determined by how busy you are. Each item we carry has a minimum reorder quantity based on how quickly the product turns and how many baskets it is included in.

For example, our supply of 250 ml containers of antipasto is marked as Item #SRA01. There are 12 units per case, and we know to reorder when the stock reaches 48 units. During our busy cruise ship season or at Christmas, the minimum reorder number is increased. (Further details regarding inventory control and accounting can be found in chapter 12.)

h. Establishing Terms and Credit

If you are starting up a new business, it can take a little time to establish a credit rating, as you will not have trade references and your bank may not give you a credit rating if your account has just opened. Be prepared to pay C.O.D. (cash on delivery) for most of your opening inventory. Many suppliers of gift basket merchandise also accept credit cards, which gives you 20 to 30 days to pay depending on when you make the purchase.

After you have been dealing with a supplier on a C.O.D. basis for a few orders, the supplier will probably be willing to give you credit.

Once you have established accounts with three suppliers, it should be easy to open accounts with other suppliers as long as you pay your bills.

Many suppliers will give additional discounts when you pay with cash at the time of the purchase, and it is standard to receive a 2% discount if you pay your invoice in ten days. Following are the terms of credit with one basket manufacturer, which are not untypical:

Terms of credit

- Cash or company check and product taken at time of purchase: 8% discount

- Credit card payment and product taken at time of purchase: 5% discount

- Net 30 days and product taken at time of purchase: 3% discount

- Net 30 days and product delivered — no discount

As you can see, some of those discounts can add up to large savings if you have the cash flow to take advantage of them.

When choosing suppliers, you need to consider where they are located and how much the freight can add on to your cost of goods if they are being shipped in from a long distance.

When placing orders with out-of-town suppliers, place your orders well in advance to take advantage of the slowest and least expensive form of shipping.

Most suppliers have minimum purchase requirements. A $100 minimum order is standard in the industry and opening orders can sometimes be as high as $250, which is to help offset the supplier's costs in opening a new account. Suppliers will also have minimum quantities of a particular item, usually case packs of 12 or more, which can make it difficult for some smaller businesses just starting out. Recently there have been a number of companies selling small quantities of gift basket supplies at a slightly higher than wholesale price. Most of these companies have displays at the major gift shows and dealing with them can be a good option for a new business.

i. Setting a Price for Your Product

For a new businessperson who is trying to attract customers but, of course, make a profit, it is always difficult to know where to set your prices. You want to be competitive, but you need to have a firm handle on your costs as well. If your price is too high, you meet with price resistance and the customer won't buy your product. If your price is too low, the customer might assume the goods are cheap or poorly made and refuse to buy for that reason. Striking a balance and making a profit is the challenge.

There are a few pricing options you might consider.

1. *100% mark-up*

First you need to determine a selling price for your gift basket based on your costs. Consider the example that was used in the previous chapter:

Basket: "Gourmet Treasures"
Basket or container — $4
Mineral water — $1.25
Brie cheese — $2.60
Pâté — $3
Antipasto — $2.40
Water crackers — $1.30
Chocolates — $4
Pâté/cheese spreader — $.50
Cocktail napkins — $.50
Packaging — $1.45
Total cost — $21
Selling price — $42

When your selling price is double your total cost, your gross profit margin is 50% and your mark-up is 100%.

Mark-up and gross profit margin are often confused. When expressed as a percentage, gross profit margin is figured as a percentage of the selling price, and mark-up is figured as a percentage of the seller's cost. Use the following equation to figure your mark-up percentage:

(Total sales – cost of sales ÷ cost of sales)

Using the figures from the basket sample above, this is how you compute your mark-up:

Total sales = $42
Minus cost of sales =$21
Divided by cost of sales =$21
= 100% mark-up

This is the easiest and most common way to set a price for a gift basket. Depending how and where the delivery is to be made, it may be necessary to add a handling and delivery charge to the total.

2. Wholesale costing

You can also calculate your price by doubling the wholesale cost price of the contents of the basket and charging the container and materials at cost with a 10% to 20% charge for labor. This option can be useful when using a more expensive container which would make the price of the basket prohibitive if you doubled the cost of the entire package. For example:

Container = $20 wholesale cost
Contents = $25 wholesale cost
Materials = $5 wholesale cost

Using this method, you would price the basket at $75 plus 20% labor, which equals $15, for a total retail price of $90. If you use this method, remember to include the cost of freight or delivery of the products to your location into the wholesale cost price.

3. Pricing large volume orders

If you start to deal with corporate clients who are ordering in quantity, you will want to offer some type of discount in order to stay competitive. For orders of 20 or more baskets, you may be asked to give a quantity discount.

Keep in mind that making gift baskets is a very labor-intensive business and it is essential to your profitability to include cost of labor into your prices for volume orders. If you give a discount, it should be on the price of goods, containers, and materials, which is where you should be able to negotiate a better price with your suppliers. For example:

Quantity: 75 gift baskets
Cost of container, product, and materials = $25
Retail price = $50
Less 20% volume discount = $40

Plus 10% labor = $4
Total retail price = $44
Net profit per basket = $15 plus $4 labor
= $19 each x 75 = $1,425

4. Other considerations

After you have figured out how much each basket costs you, you also need to consider other factors. How sensitive is your market? The price of your product should be readily accepted by your intended customers.

What does your competition charge? You can't ignore what is perceived as the going rate for a product or service unless you can prove that your product offers a definite advantage.

Keep all these factors in mind after you have figured your costs with the above equations.

j. Computing Your Profit Margin

Cost of goods sold or cost of sales refers to the cost of products for resale. Gross profit margin or gross margin is the difference between net sales (total sales less any discounts) and the cost of goods sold. For example:

Net sale	$500
Cost of sales	$250
Gross margin	$250

Gross margin can be expressed in either dollars or as a percentage. As a percentage, the gross margin is stated as a percentage of net sales. Use the following equation to figure your gross profit margin percentage:

(Net sales – cost of sales ÷ net sales)

In the above example, the gross margin would be 50% ($500 – $250 ÷ $500).

After all operating expenses (utilities, insurance, advertising, office supplies, rent, salaries, etc.) are deducted from the gross profit margin, what remains is your net profit before taxes. Operating expenses can vary tremendously from one operation to another. It is possible to operate a profitable company on a much lower gross profit margin than the 50% shown above and still end up with a good net profit before taxes.

Chapter 7
KEEPING YOUR OPERATIONS IN ORDER

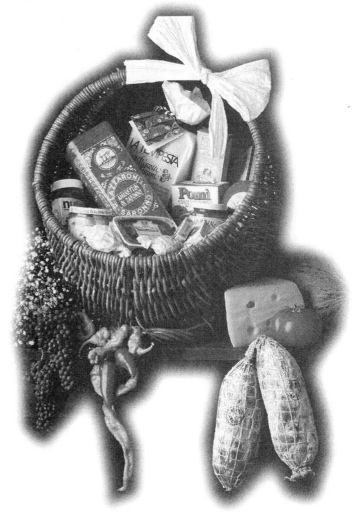

a. Striking a Balance

Most new gift basket companies are generally a one-person operation. Be prepared to put in long hours when starting out. You will likely put in 50 to 60 hours each week if you are starting up a full-time business. You will be doing everything from making the baskets and ordering merchandise to keeping records and collecting payment.

It is easy in a business like this one to spend all your time on the creative end at the expense of record keeping. You can't afford to let those details get out of hand; you need to know whether you are making or losing money. On the other hand, don't forget that you also need to be out marketing, advertising, and selling — not behind your computer all day figuring out detailed financial projections. You need to strike a balance to keep your business running smoothly and profitably.

b. Hours of Operation

Set your hours of operation to allow you to do out-of-office business early in the morning or later in the day. If you operate your business from 10:00 a.m. to 4:00 p.m. daily, for example, you will still have three business hours of the day to make deliveries, do banking, and pick up stock.

As I have stated previously, the most important place for you to be is in your place of business. If you use a reliable courier company, delivery company, shipping company, and make arrangements to have inventory shipped to your place of business, it should not be necessary for you to be out of the workplace that often.

It is also important to you and your business that you have a personal life, especially if you have decided to operate your business out of your home. If you are running the business by yourself, operate it during the weekdays only and take the weekends off. If some aspect of your business involves weekend deliveries, find a delivery company that works on weekends or hire a student to make them. One area of my company involves delivering gifts to cruise ships that leave port seven days a week. We make up our weekend deliveries on Friday and arrange to have them delivered by an independent company or part-time worker on the weekend.

c. Sales

The majority of your sales will be made over the telephone. The order may be for one of your standard published gift packages, or your customer may want you to design a custom package.

You can keep your sales process very efficient if you keep a binder of order forms at your desk and a complete list of the containers you have available, as well as all of the stock items that you carry and their prices. It is also helpful to have a listing of wines and liquor and their prices. Keep the rates for local courier delivery and for out-of-town shipping nearby, along with a calculator, so you can easily give the customer a total price.

Sample 7 shows the order form I use for taking a gift package order from cruise ship clients.

Keep these order forms permanently in a binder. This is the information you will use to generate an invoice. You will also put this information into your data base for future customer mailings. If your client is looking for a custom-made gift, ask the following questions:

(a) What is the occasion for giving the gift?

(b) Is the recipient male or female?

(c) What age group is the recipient?

(d) Does the recipient have any dietary restrictions (e.g., vegetarian, allergies, kosher, doesn't drink)?

(e) Does the recipient have any special interests or hobbies (e.g., cooking, gardening, wine appreciation)?

(f) What is the client's budget?

FOSTER WALKER
ENTERPRISES INC.

Alaska - Canada Cruise Gift Services

TWO ORDERS PER FORM

Fax orders to: 1- 800- 668- 6855

Date:	Contact:
Phone:	Fax:
Agency:	Foster-Walker Enterprises Account number:
Address:	

1. Item no	Description	Qty	Total	2. Item no	Description	Qty	Total
			$				$
			$				$
			$				$
			$				$
			$				$
			$				$
			$				$

☐ More order forms/price lists required   ☐ More order forms/price lists required

Total order 1   Prices include taxes and delivery $ Total order 2   Prices include taxes and delivery $

Port of Embarkation: Vancouver	Port of Embarkation: Vancouver
Ship:	Ship:
Sailing date:	Sailing date:
Cabin number:	Cabin number:
Passenger name(s):	Passenger name(s):
Your personal message:	Your personal message:

Total Payment: **Payment by way of:**

☐ Cheque (check)   ☐ or Money Order

payable to Foster Walker Enterprises Inc. (must be mailed on the same date as order is faxed, unless you have set up an account with us) OR:

Please charge my: ☐ Visa   ☐ Mastercard   ☐ American Express

Card number:	Expiry date:
Name on card:	Signature of cardholder:

Note: All prices in budget friendly Canadian dollars.

Special Requests:

Foster Walker Enterprises Inc.
201-1200 West Pender Street
Vancouver B.C. Canada V6E 2S9
Phone: (toll free) 1- 800- 668-8813
Phone: (604) 681- 2456
Fax: (604) 681- 2003

Help your clients become successful gift givers. Listen and give advice. They would not be calling if they had the time or creativity to select the perfect gift themselves. If you are meeting with the customer in person, show samples or pictures of your baskets. If you are selling over the phone, be as graphic as possible about your products. Creativity is key and coming up with the perfect gift for your client to give is essential to building long-term customers. Following are some tips:

(a) Keep the recipient in mind when helping to select a gift. What are the recipient's interests, lifestyle, age, line of work, etc.?

(b) Always have your client include a personal message.

(c) Giving a well-selected gift a few weeks before the holidays (especially if it can be used for entertaining) will be much more meaningful. The first gifts of the season are more readily remembered.

(d) Suggest that your client give several of the same object. The gift's impact is dramatically increased by duplicating it in several colors, styles, or designs — a basket of different size picture frames, or taper candles, a selection of choice olive oils, coffees, teas, or preserves are some examples.

(e) Suggest that your client create an annual gift-giving occasion, one that relates to the recipient's interests, heritage, or profession: Louis Armstrong's birthday, Beethoven's birthday, International Yo Yo Day, Mardi Gras, Bastille Day, the Spring Equinox — the possibilities are endless.

(f) Suggest combining items. A gift becomes more distinctive and personal when paired with something that individualizes it: a basket of spices with a spice grinder and cookbook, theater tickets with a bottle of champagne in an ice bucket, tickets to a sporting event in a tailgate picnic basket. If your client has a copy of your published brochure, then he or she should already have a good indication of what your gift packages will cost. When designing custom baskets, give your clients three or four options in various price points. You may be surprised at the number of times you can sell them on the more expensive gift. Unless they have a very limited budget, many clients are willing to spend a little extra for something unique.

Ideally it is best to have a couple of days to complete the order, but often your clients will be ordering at the last minute and it will be necessary to turn the gift around very quickly. For this reason, it is important to have inventory on hand.

d. Payment

There are a few options to consider for taking payment for your services:

(a) Cash on delivery

(b) Credit cards

(c) Invoicing

1. Cash on delivery

If your customer picks up the gift in person or you deliver the gift to a home or office, he or she can pay you at the time of purchase by cash or check. You may want to keep a small cash float on hand in your petty cash box to make change for cash purchases as well as a receipt book to use when making this type of transaction. If you deliver the gift to them, you will need to take change and a receipt book.

2. Credit cards

It is common for gift basket companies to take orders over the phone and have the customer pay for the gift by credit card. Even small home-based businesses should try to set up with at least one credit card system. Most home-based or office/studio gift basket operators never even see their customers because the majority of business is done over the phone or fax, so offering payment options by credit card is a real plus for your customers.

You may want to start out by taking either Visa or MasterCard, depending on which card your bank supports. You might consider opening an American Express account at a later date — especially if your corporate clients grow in number.

The bank charge or commission on credit cards can run as high as 4% or 5%, but if you do some research into memberships of local business organizations, you can save on that amount. Your local Chamber of Commerce, Board of Trade, merchants association, tourism association, etc. offer members substantially reduced credit card commission rates. The fee for joining these organizations really pays for itself because you can take advantage of such membership benefits. Do your research before you open your doors for business.

When taking payment by credit card, ask the customer which credit card he or she wants to use. Take the card number, expiration date, and the full name of the person the card is issued to. All telephone credit card transactions must be phoned in for authorization regardless of your floor limit (the dollar amount that the credit card company sets for authorization if the customer is present to sign the card).

Phone and have the card authorized before you send out the gift. In order to protect yourself, it is a wise idea to have the customer fax you his or her signature authorizing you to accept payment on the card. Credit card fraud is a major problem and it may be necessary for you to always have a customer signature before a bank will allow you to open a credit card account. Many banks will no longer open new commercial credit card merchant accounts if they suspect that cards may be taken without a signature.

In all my years in business, I have never had a situation where someone tried to order a gift basket on a stolen credit card, but the credit card companies are now extremely careful about opening new merchant accounts.

3. Invoicing

Once you have established regular repeat clients and corporate accounts, they will expect you to invoice them. Many large companies are not set up to pay for gift purchases on credit cards or by cash. Most businesses issue checks twice a month and if you want to deal with that type of client (and you most definitely do) you must be prepared to invoice them and wait for payment. I have never had a client who I invoiced not pay me, which is probably because most companies who are solvent enough to order gifts also are in the financial position to pay their bills.

When invoicing a client you should always put the terms of payment on the invoice. Normally these terms would be payable on receipt of invoice and payable net 10 days (or 15 or 30 days) depending on the terms you have negotiated with your client.

Unless I have been specifically asked for certain terms, I almost always say the terms are payable on receipt of invoice. If the accounts clerk at the company you are billing sees this on an invoice, he or she is more likely to issue you payment during the next check run. See Sample 8 for an example of an invoice.

ENTERPRISES INC.

INVOICE # 1187   INVOICE # 1187

To:	ABC Tours ATTN: Jane Smith
	001 West George St.
	Vancouver, BC
	V6C 2W6
From:	FOSTER-WALKER ENTERPRISES INC.
	Suite 201, 1200 West Pender Street,
	Vancouver, BC V6E 2S9
RE:	Gift Baskets DATE: November 14, 1994
TERMS:	Payable on receipt of invoice

2 Gift Baskets @ $25.00 each $ 50.00

SUB-TOTAL	$ 50.00
7% GST	3.50
7% PST	3.50
TOTAL DUE	$ 57.00

GST #R138372677
THANK YOU FOR YOUR PATRONAGE. WE ARE PLEASED TO HAVE BEEN OF
SERVICE TO YOU.

201-1200 West Pender Street
Vancouver, B.C. Canada V6E 2S9
Phone: (toll free) 1-800-668-8813
Fax: (toll free) 1-800-668-6855
Phone: (604) 681-2456
Fax: (604) 681-2003

*Note: Reference to GST and PST are for Canadians only. Substitute the appropriate state tax, if applicable.

e. Keeping Your Nonfinancial Records in Order

All of your day-to-day operations, as described above, will generate a lot of paperwork that will need to be organized and that must be maintained. Just as you don't want the paperwork to overwhelm you, you also don't want to forget about it completely. Keeping good administrative records can improve efficiency and profit. Nonfinancial records and office systems should be maintained efficiently and updated consistently. Office systems should be implemented to reduce exposure to liability and to increase your awareness of how well the business is running.

1. Calendars

Important dates and deadlines should be entered into an effective calendar system (see section **f.** on time management and setting priorities). An effective calendar system will provide adequate lead time on various activities (gearing up for the Christmas season, arranging for advertising, etc.) and follow up to ensure that all the tasks have been performed.

2. Filing systems

Take the time to develop an effective filing system to eliminate the possibility of misplacing order forms or invoices. A filing reference system should be designed so you can easily retrieve information on a client or an account when needed.

3. Billing, credit, and collection

As discussed above, you need to keep on top of your billing and invoicing. Monthly or interim billing should be done wherever possible if your clients are not paying immediately. This means bills can be sent close to the time the work was done. It also keeps your cash flow even and enables you to spot any discrepancies. An effective record-keeping system for credit and collection is also needed.

4. Personnel records

If you hire casual help from time to time — perhaps in your busy season, or if your business grows to the point that you hire a regular employee — you will need to keep personnel records. These contain all documents and correspondence relating to an employee from the time of applying for employment to termination. Individual employee records also include a summary of personal data, education and training, work history, and job and wage record.

5. Tax records

Tax records record details of sales taxes, income taxes, business taxes, and employee income tax deductions. Most businesses are regulated by a combination of federal, state/ provincial, and local governments. The information for these records is obtained from different aspects of the business operation. For example, payroll deductions are obtained from the payroll records, and information on sales taxes collected comes from either the sales journal or the daily summary of your sales and cash receipts.

f. Managing Your Time

Time management is an essential skill in a business that is busier during some seasons than others. Sensible time management begins by setting priorities, and that will affect all aspects of your business.

The first year of your business is a busy one. There are many steps necessary on the way to your success. As you begin to receive orders for gift baskets, deal with suppliers, keep books and records, etc., demands for your time will escalate.

It's a good idea to organize your agenda from the very beginning. It helps to divide it into three segments: long term, intermediate, and immediate. Define each segment of time in whatever way you like. For example, your long-term agenda could be a year or it could be six months if you find that time frame works better for you.

1. The long-term agenda

The foundation of time management is list making — setting down what you are going to do and when you plan to do it. Begin by deciding how long your long term is to be, and then make a list of activities required in that time period.

You will find that assigning priority to the activities takes some thought, and it is easier to list what has to be done first and worry about ranking later. The main purpose of your agenda is to consider every possibility. Make your list as complete as you can.

2. The intermediate agenda

Your long-term agenda likely runs to more than one page if it is as complete as it should be. You begin to refine your agenda when you do the intermediate section. Start by reviewing every item on the long-term list. If you have chosen six months as your intermediate period, transfer all the things that need to be accomplished in this time frame to a new list.

3. The immediate agenda

Now you can create your immediate agenda. Follow the same procedure you used for your intermediate agenda. Scan your list and transfer all activities that require prompt attention to your new list. If you have designated one week as the time period of your immediate agenda, look for dates that fall within that period. Write all the activities for that time span on the new list. Enter them by order of date.

If you wish, you can bypass the immediate agenda and enter your planned activities in your business diary. If you do this, don't forget to estimate the allocated time.

4. Learning your turnaround time

Having several days' notice to complete a gift order is ideal, but as I have previously stated, that is not always the case. Be prepared to complete baskets on very short notice. It is not uncommon to take an order for a gift basket in the morning that needs to be delivered that afternoon. When this happens, it may be necessary to charge the client a rush charge.

Use the steps set out below to help you set your long-term, intermediate, and immediate priorities. For example, I send out my December holidays gift brochure at the end of October and follow up with phone calls in November (but we still end up with last-minute orders on December 24!). Generally clients who are placing large orders will give you plenty of lead time because they can't expect you to turn around large orders in just a few days. Having good local sources of gift basket inventory is essential for your first year in business. After you have been in business for a while and you have a good indication of what sells and how much you need, ordering from more distant suppliers will be feasible.

5. Time management systems

If setting priorities isn't your strong suit, you can rely on some already-tested systems. Walk into any office stationery shop and you will find a selection of calendars, diaries, and time-management systems for sale. All are designed to help you get and stay organized.

If you are already comfortable on a computer, there are some excellent systems available that offer calendars, memo capability, and extensive list-making facilities. Day sheets and plans can be printed for your convenience. One of the good things about computerized systems is that they don't let you forget. Once you enter an item on your "things to do" list, the computer will automatically carry the item forward until you indicate that it is done.

g. Consumer Fairs and Trade Shows

Your time will also be taken up by attending some of the many consumer fairs and trade shows that are offered in your community. Consumer fairs are open to the public and generally last for several days over a weekend. Trade shows are generally targeted to a specific market and can be from one to three or four days in duration.

During the year, attend as many of these shows as possible to ascertain which would be appropriate for your business. Examples of a consumer fair would be a home and garden show or a Christmas craft fair. The organizers of the fair advertise to the public in newspapers, magazines, and on radio and television. Participants pay a fee to take a booth to display their products or services.

An example of a trade show would be one that is targeted toward a particular industry, such as a show for cruise-only travel agents. The people organizing the show invite the people they want to attend, and the participants pay a fee to have a booth to display their products and services.

The cost of booth space at these shows can be expensive, and I suggest you wait until after your first year of operation before committing the time and money to being an exhibitor at any fair. If you are considering getting involved in this type of marketing venture, make sure the show is reputable, has had success over a period of a few years, has extensive advertising and mailing lists, and can guarantee you a certain number of participants.

h. Staying Organized As You Grow

With good promotional materials and advertising, it will not take long for your business to flourish, and at some point you will need to hire extra help.

Even in the early stages of your new business, it is wise to have extra help organized on a casual basis. These people may be students who are available to work evenings, weekends, or during school breaks or homemakers who may not be prepared to commit to regular time or full-time jobs but who will work occasionally when they don't have family commitments. Having this type of employee to call on is essential for the new business owner and will be a lifesaver when large orders start to come in. (Employment options are covered in further detail in chapter 10 on employees and personnel.)

One of the most difficult decisions a small business owner must make is when to bring in help and hire employees. Do not fall into the trap of trying to save money by doing all the work yourself. The point of starting a business is to grow and prosper. If you don't hire people to help you when the business warrants it, you risk producing low-quality merchandise, missing deadlines, and not providing good service. Do not put all of the hard work you have put into your business at risk by not knowing when it is time to grow.

As your business grows and becomes financially feasible, hire a part-time or full-time assistant to take over some aspect of the business. Personally, I prefer looking after the more creative side of my company and having an employee take care of the bookkeeping, invoicing, banking, check writing, data base updating, etc. Find the balance that is right for you — and for your business.

Chapter 8
ADVERTISING AND PROMOTION

a. Why You Should Advertise

Gifts and gift packages do not sell themselves without some kind of promotion, advertising, and marketing. In time, an established business may rely more on word-of-mouth advertising, but for a new company starting up, it is essential to put some dollars aside for an advertising and marketing budget. Many businesses allocate 2% to 5% of their projected gross sales as an advertising budget. For example, if your projected gross sales for the first year are $200,000 based on your business plan, you would have $10,000 or about $835 per month to spend. For your opening promotion, you would allocate $1,670, which is standard in the industry. (See Sample 13 at the end of this chapter for a breakdown of advertising and promotion expenses.)

Even if your business is in a small community, there will be companies that will need your services: insurance companies, real estate offices and agents, banks, development firms, law offices, medical offices, manufacturers, auto sales and leasing companies, hotels, travel agents, investment firms, etc. The key is letting these companies know about your gift basket business with direct marketing by mail and by telephone, and by making appointments to show your products and services. Do not be discouraged if your hard work does not generate immediate sales. A major corporate order could take up to six months to come your way.

The purpose of advertising is to inform current and prospective customers about your services which enables you to —

(a) showcase your products and services and show why they are superior to the competition,

(b) enhance your company's image,

(c) create a need and desire for your products and show the ease of doing business with you,

(d) promote new products, and

(e) establish new customers.

Good advertising should have the following components:

(a) It should be easily understood.

(b) It should be truthful.

(c) It should be informative.

(d) It should be sincere.

(e) It should be customer-oriented.

(f) It should tell who, what, when, where, why, and how.

b. Print Media

A successful advertising program is a long-term commitment that grows and shows a return over time. It makes better sense to put your advertising budget to use in a consistent, repetitive program and take out small advertisements on a regular basis, than to put all of your dollars into large, infrequent advertisements.

Choosing the medium or type of advertising can be especially difficult for a small business. Television, radio, major newspapers, and magazines with large circulations are too expensive for most small businesses just starting out. However, smaller newspaper and magazine publications can be highly effective and much more economical. If you decide to run an advertising program in a newspaper or magazine, I recommend running ads in a six-week series if they are dailies or weeklies and running an ad for six months straight if it is a monthly publication.

Obviously, when you choose to run ads will depend on the type of market that you are going after and the season of gift giving. Most gift basket companies advertise during the December holiday season, as well as at Valentine's, Easter, Mother's Day, and Father's Day.

To select the publications you want to advertise in, you first need to define your goals and analyze them in terms of budget to determine the best print medium to reach your target market. Your effective print advertising program may involve an overlap between news-letters, regional magazines, newspapers, and the Yellow Pages. Study your competition to find out how they are advertising, and look for alternatives to make your ads unique and more effective.

Your public library should be an excellent source of researching all the publications that are available for you to advertise in. Make a list of the publications that interest you and then contact them. Set up appointments with one of their salespersons and obtain a media kit from each publication. These kits will give you the advertising rates as well as the circulation and demographics. Determine the cost effectiveness of advertising in the publication by the circulation rates.

CPM (cost per thousand) is the industry standard for determining the cost effectiveness by circulation. For example, if the circulation is 40,000 and the rate for a full page ad is $800, you would divide the cost by 40. In this case you would have a $20 cost per thousand.

c. Direct Mail

Volumes have been written on the subject of direct mail advertising, and it seems to be a popular medium with many gift packaging companies. Direct mail can be effective for all sizes of business, from a small home-based operation to large retail chains. It must be thoughtfully worded to create the impression of individual attention to each recipient.

As a new business, you will not have a large customer data base and mailing list, so it may be necessary to purchase one if you want to advertise through direct mail. There are many companies in the business of selling lists and they may be found in the Yellow Pages under the headings Advertising or Direct Mail. The company you select will help you choose the right mailing list for you. You can purchase the list on computer disk so you can print the addresses on your envelopes or mailing labels and merge the names on your personal letter, written on your company letterhead.

Enclose your sales piece with the personal letter and send it by first-class mail. Anything less will be perceived as junk mail and will be a waste of your time and money.

Following are some tips for using direct mail marketing:

(a) Target your prospect list carefully so that you are contacting only those who are most likely to need your products.

(b) Design the material to be mailed. Make use of professional designers as needed (see section **e.** below) and use the following guidelines:

- Use descriptive headings.
- Keep paragraphs short.
- Retain a lot of white space.
- Use color.
- Get to the point.
- Capture attention early.
- Establish the product's uniqueness.
- Direct the reader to do something.
- Keep it simple.
- Offer something.
- Set a time limit.
- Use guarantees.
- Use testimonials.
- Personalize the piece.
- Include a fax-back order form.
- Include a self-addressed postage paid envelope to encourage a return.

(c) Do your mailing soon after purchasing your prospect list; 20% of business information changes each month.

(d) Mail often. The direct marketing association claims that the fifth mailing attracts 25% more interest than the first. Depending on how targeted your first mailing is, expect from 2% to 5% response.

(e) Follow up mailings with a phone call.

(f) Choose the time of your mailing carefully. Avoid dead times such as summer vacation, between Christmas and New Year's, tax time, etc.

(g) When a potential client responds to your mailing, follow up immediately.

See Sample 9 for an example of a direct mail sales piece my company uses.

d. The Yellow Pages

Just about everybody in business advertises in the Yellow Pages. Advertisements vary from simple, one-line listings to half-page ads with spot color and graphics. Budget to place a display ad as large as you can afford and have it professionally designed (see section **e.** below). Choose the most appropriate categories to be listed under; you may want to consider advertising in more than one category.

Be sure you understand the region for the Yellow Pages, as several different regional versions of the Yellow Pages may be published in a large, metropolitan area. Yellow Pages in most places are published only once a year, so don't forget to send in your ad by the deadline. Normally you will receive one free regular listing in the category of your choice, but additional listings or display ads cost extra. Gift Baskets would be the obvious choice for one listing, and you may want to also take listings under Gifts, Promotional Items, Convention Services, and Baskets.

Here are some statistics that Yellow Pages advertises:

- Your ad is available in every home and office 24 hours a day, 365 days a year.

- 85% of adults have used the Yellow Pages at least once in the last four weeks.

- 82% contact at least one business after using the Yellow Pages.

- 66% made a purchase after referring to the Yellow Pages.

- 45% of those making a purchase had never dealt with that business before.

e. Professional Design Services

Unless you have some experience in art or design, don't be tempted to create your own advertising or direct mail pieces. While graphic design computer programs are now available that make creative pieces more accessible to everyone, I feel it is a mistake to cut corners when it comes to your professional image. You must remember that you are trying to attract the attention of a diverse group of potential

SAMPLE 9
DIRECT MAIL SALES PIECE

Front

CORPORATE GIFTS • CONVENTION GIFTS • ALASKA CRUISE GIFTS • PROMOTIONAL MERCHANDISE • UNIQUE GIFT PACKAGES & BASKETS

Let us make you look good on Time & on Budget.

Back

CORPORATE GIFTS • CONVENTION GIFTS • ALASKA CRUISE GIFTS • PROMOTIONAL MERCHANDISE • UNIQUE GIFT PACKAGES & BASKETS

Gifts of Distinction

We will find the perfect gift to suit your budget and take care of all the details of gift wrapping, packaging and delivery.

From pre-conference mailers, delegate amenities, promotional items, welcome packages to speaker gifts and awards.

There is no other Gift Company that can come close to our: Quality, Service & Pricing.

Please send your full colour Corporate Brochure to:

Name:

Title:

Company:

Address:

Phone:

Fax:

FOSTER WALKER ENTERPRISES INC.

Tel: (604) 681-2456   or toll free   1-800-668-8813
Fax: (604) 681-2003   or toll free   1-800-668-6855

FOSTER WALKER
ENTERPRISES INC.
201 - 1200 West Pender Street
Vancouver, B.C.
Canada V6E 2S9

clients, from the "person on the street" who may buy an individual gift basket from time to time, to the more lucrative business accounts who are used to highly polished presentations in advertising.

You don't have to spend money on a large advertising agency, but you should hire a professional — but affordable — designer to work on your advertising and marketing program. Smaller firms and independent graphic designers are less expensive and will often do work at reasonable rates because they want to build up their portfolios. If you cannot afford to hire a designer, ask around and find friends with desktop design skills or find students who need experience.

Before meeting with any designer, do your homework and find out what it costs to print business cards, letterhead, envelopes, labels, and brochures. Find out the prices for professional photography and color printing. Make it clear when meeting with the designer that you will pay for design fees only, and that you will deal directly with the printers and photographer. If the designer quotes a flat fee, ask that it be broken down into the various design components. Work out a reasonable payment schedule and suggest the opportunity for a full or partial contract for your gift services.

The best source for finding a good graphic designer is by referral from other businesses. When you start your market research, collect brochures and advertising pieces that appeal to you and find out who did the design work. Make appointments to meet with several designers to look at their portfolios and see if you can afford to hire them.

This is the person who will design your letterhead, business cards, brochure, and advertising, so it is important that the two of you get along personally. A good working relationship with a talented graphic designer can be invaluable and can save you a lot of time and money.

Have a clear idea of what you want before working with a designer. The more research you do prior to hiring a designer, the less it will cost you. Visit your local art supply store and purchase a book of type styles, fonts, and computer graphics. Choose in advance the ones that match the look you are after. The more direction you can give the designer, the less time he or she will have to spend on your project, thus saving you money.

Hiring a professional graphic artist to design your printed materials is probably the most important investment you can make in starting up your new business, and having quality printed materials can definitely make a difference in sales. Keep in mind that the cost of printing poorly designed stationery and sales pieces is the same as printing well-designed and effective ones.

f. Names and Logos

What to call your new company and how to design your company logo are two of the more important decisions you will make.

1. A name that sells

Most professionals agree that your company name should describe your products and services. When deciding on a name consider the following points:

(a) Where will your company name be when printed in the telephone directory, Yellow Pages, or other alphabetical listing?

(b) Is the name easy to spell and pronounce?

(c) Is the name easy to say?

(d) How does the name sound over the telephone?

(e) Is the name too long?

(f) Is the name too cute? (I know of several gift basket company names that sound more like escort services!)

(g) Will your name be limiting to you in the future? (Think ahead. If you decide in the future to expand, don't be stuck with a name that is limiting to what your business has become.)

If you decide to use all or part of your own name, you should combine it with something descriptive of your business. Of course, you also have to keep in mind certain legal restrictions that limit your choice of business name. The legal aspects of choosing a business name are discussed in chapter 11.

2. A logo that tells

Your logo should be graphically pleasing and should also visually describe the services you offer.

As part of an advertising seminar I once participated in, we were asked to identify 20 graphic logos of large international corporations. Most of the participants were only able to match a few of the logos with the correct company. The lesson here is that your company is probably not going to become a Sony or McDonald's, and you should keep your company image simple and descriptive.

g. Image

Your company image should have a professional and competent quality to reflect the services you provide. If your advertising and sales materials look and feel of high quality, your customers can only assume that the products you provide will be of the same caliber. You must then decide what type of image you want to project in the design of your piece. How do you want to be perceived? Who is your potential customer? Is the image of your piece:

Country — Nostalgic — Whimsical,

Sophisticated — Big City — Elegant, or

High Tech — Modern — Contemporary?

By this point you should have a large collection of brochures and advertising pieces that are similar in feel and design to the image you are trying to attain. Have a clear picture of that image before you hire a professional to work with you to make sure you hire the right person for the design project.

h. Design and Copy

Once you have hired the right designer, you are ready to begin the design process. Your designer should provide several variations of the look you are trying to attain. At this point, you should also hire a professional copywriter to fine-tune the written information. The more written information you can provide the copywriter, the less time he or she will have to spend on the project, thus costing you less money.

See Sample 10 for a sample layout of the classic five-point design for a display ad in print media. Statistics show that over 90% of the ads run in national magazines use this design.

i. Color and Photography

I am a firm believer in the use of color and photography to sell products. Potential clients want to see what the products look like and your only way to reach customers is through the use of a sales and marketing piece. How many people would buy something they have not seen?

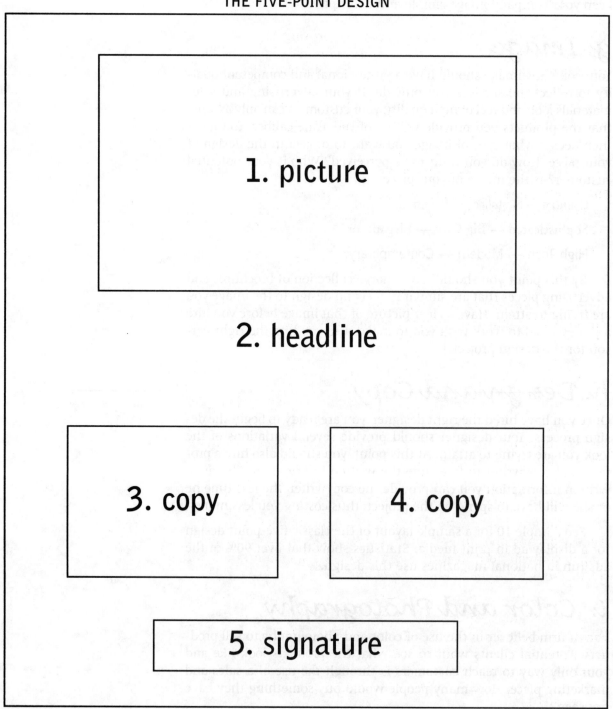

1. picture

2. headline

3. copy

4. copy

5. signature

Mail order is one of the fastest growing businesses in North America, but I cannot think of one successful mail order company that does not use full color photography to sell its merchandise. In the past, the use of color photographic advertising pieces was too costly for many small companies, but with recent advancements in printing technology, it is possible to have full color photographic sales materials produced. From my own experience, I was amazed at the almost instant increase in sales when I had my first professionally designed full color photographic sales brochure produced.

j. Sales Brochure

The single most important item you will invest in is your sales brochure and marketing kit, and unless you are a trained graphic artist, copywriter, and photographer, you should hire professionals to help you put it together. The best way to find these people is by referral.

Find brochures and sales pieces that have good design and photography and contact the company's sales and marketing department to find out who did the work for them. Ask if they were happy with the price and if the designer was on time and on budget.

Have three different design firms and photographers quote on your job. Even though the design company will want to look after the photography and the printing, in the long run it will save you considerably to look after each of the components yourself.

Sample 11 shows the cover and inside pages of the sales brochure for my company. The back cover is blank except for my logo and address.

1. Set up the photography session

Determine how many items you want to photograph and which ones could work together in a grouping. Then decide how many photographs you will need in total. Six to eight is a standard number of photographs for a gift company brochure.

Look at the examples of the photographer's work and discuss what type of props, style, and lighting you are aiming for. Offer to be there on the day of the shoot to assist and make sure the products are being photographed correctly. Your helping out will keep the price lower since an extra assistant will be unnecessary.

$\mathscr{F}$OSTER $\mathscr{W}$ALKER

ENTERPRISES INC.

Convention, Corporate, Cruise,

Gift services.

Gifts with distinction

A gift. A token. A way to say Bon Voyage, thank you for your business, or thank you for making our business better. Every person, every situation is unique. At Foster-Walker Enterprises we combine the skill of the best caterers, florists and artisans to provide exquisite custom hampers, baskets and floral arrangements. For example, fulfill your most romantic expectations with our deluxe custom designed picnic hamper as seen on the front cover, which comes complete with your choice of wine, glasses, fresh flowers, gourmet foods, candles, picnic linens and blanket! Whether it is a delicacy to be savoured or a keepsake to be treasured, Foster-Walker Enterprises is in the business of recognizing individual contributions with memorable gifts, specifically chosen for each and every occasion.

Baskets they'll remember

Gift-boxed 10 oz. moose mug filled with assorted goodies, Native design woven mat with a variety of delightful gourmet snacks, scenic watercolour design luncheon mat with a selection of picnic treats, nostalgia wood crate brimming with delicacies for the ultimate picnic.

Fresh floral arrangements, fresh ideas

Choose from a natural wood basket, Native design box with killer whale lid, Native design round box with bear mask lid, or Native design killer whale bowl, all filled with a bouquet of mixed seasonal blooms.

Books – for lasting memories

A range of titles to suit the occasion, from hard cover coffee table picture books, to pocket calendars for the prospective traveller. Useful references for the journey and the perfect souvenir to remember the sights and experiences along the way.

Lighthearted whimsy

Cruise ship coverup in 100% cotton, full-size and mini hand crafted nutcrackers in goose and mallard designs, fat faced moose basket filled with an assortment of gourmet products, moose tote bag in sturdy canvas filled with a fine selection of picnic delicacies, choose from a range of designs.

North by Northwest

Gifts and souvenirs from the Pacific Northwest. Choose from Native design potlatch blanket, bent wood boxes, gift-boxed smoked salmon, 100 year old framed photographs, jade killer whale sculpture, or Native design pewter fork and ladle, lidded boxes, totem poles, and letter opener.

When only the best will do

For that extra special souvenir or gift, select from the highest quality framed art prints, globe bowls, crystal wine decanters, Native design objets d'art and carvings in pewter, jade, hematite or wood.

Make sure your quote is in writing and that you retain ownership of the negatives for future use.

2. Meet with the graphic designer

Meet with the designer and bring examples of brochures that appeal to you. Look carefully at the designer's portfolio to determine the style of piece that you want.

Show the designer samples of the products that you will be featuring in your brochure and let him or her know how many photographs you're including in the piece.

Have the graphic artist design all of the following components:

(a) Logo/design of company name

(b) Letterhead, envelopes, and business cards

(c) Gift tags and gift label stickers

(d) Color brochure with photography

(e) Price list

(Sample 12 shows the gift tags and labels I've had designed for my company.)

Discuss what the size of the piece will be. The bigger or more unusually sized brochure that lands on the desk of your prospective client is less likely to end up in the trash basket. It may end up costing you a bit more in mailing, but in the long run it will help generate more sales.

Make sure your quote is in writing and has a time frame and deadline for the project. And always make sure you proof the material and sign it off before anything is allowed to go to the printer.

If you are on a tight budget and you or a friend are creative, it is possible to design a sales piece using some of the wonderful textured and colored papers available in graphics supplies stores. There are also a number of excellent computer programs on the market that would be helpful when trying to design a sales brochure on your own. However, I still strongly recommend having a professional designer work with you, even if it is to design a simple, one-page flyer.

You can save some money by developing your own company presentation folders. Rather than spend extra money on having a folder printed with your company logo and name, you can buy plain folders

SAMPLE 12
GIFT TAG AND LABEL

Corporate label (printed as a peel-off sticker)

Gift tag (inside)

Gift tag (front)

that match the paper stock of your other printed materials and use one of your gift basket sticker labels on the front. Buy the presentation folders that have the cuts already made for business cards.

3. Printing

You will need two different types of printers for the materials in your sales and marketing kit. Establish a relationship with a smaller printer who can do one- and two-color work, such as letterhead, envelopes, business cards, gift tags, etc. You should find a printer who is close at hand and is able to turn things around quickly.

Then meet with three or four printers who produce four-color work and get firm quotes in writing from all of them. The printing business is very competitive and you will be surprised how much the prices can vary for the same job.

Printing is complicated; make sure your price quotes include color separations (the process of separating color originals into the primary printing color components in negative or positive form) and camera-ready art (copy that is ready for photography). Your graphic designer will need to work with your printer and photographer. Always get separate quotes to avoid having the work marked up several times over.

When looking at paper stock, ask to see what it looks like with both four-color printing and one- or two-color printing. Ask for sample letterhead stock to see how it works in your computer printer.

Ask for quotes based on running several different quantities. Sometimes the price does not vary much from one quantity to the next, and it is less expensive than having to run the whole order over in a few months.

k. Internet Marketing

The Internet and the World Wide Web are names that were rarely heard in business circles just a few years ago. Today they are hard to escape, and the Internet offers a number of unique opportunities for marketing your gift basket business.

First, where a newspaper advertisement will reach a local audience and a magazine advertisement may reach a national audience, the Internet reaches a global audience. Better yet, it reaches an affluent global audience. Your promotional efforts on the Internet reach what marketers call a self-selected audience — when someone views your Web site, he or she has chosen to do so by using a search facility to find Web pages dealing with giving gifts. The Internet's global reach also means that someone living in Germany with family in Washington state can select and pay for a gift through his or her Internet connection in Germany and have it delivered to the family member in Washington — all without leaving home.

Second, when you contract to advertise in a print publication or prepare a marketing brochure to promote your business, you commit to the content early and generally cannot make last-minute changes. For example, if the price or availability of something changes the day after your advertisement appears in print or your brochure is delivered, what do you do? Place another advertisement to correct the price, or recall and reprint the brochure?

An Internet Web site can be changed by the hour or even by the minute, and the cost of making the change is usually no more than a few minutes of someone's time.

Finally, a Web site designed to sell your product and capable of processing customer orders can and will work 24 hours a day, seven days a week, in effect keeping your business "open for business" around the clock.

1. Web sites

When you contract with an Internet Service Provider (ISP) for a connection to the Internet, even the most basic package offered by the ISP will include an e-mail address and space for your own Web pages. This is enough to create (or have someone create for you) the equivalent of a printed brochure: a few pages of information about your gift basket business, some photographs of your products, and a link on one or more of the pages that will allow the reader to send you e-mail requesting more information.

If you have already paid for high-quality photographs of your gift baskets and have written promotional copy for your print brochure, you're half way to creating your own site. With some modification, you can use these same elements on your Web page — and save on the cost of having a Web designer start your site from scratch.

If you have the budget, you will want to consider adding software to your Web pages that allows visitors to choose one or more products, select how many of each are required, and then place an order using a credit card. With the right software, such a site will verify and process the credit card immediately and provide you with the details required for shipping.

One drawback is that such a site needs quite a lot of maintenance. You need to keep it up-to-date and fresh so that repeat visitors do not get the "been there, seen that" sensation.

2. E-mail

Electronic mail, or e-mail was one of the very first applications on the Internet. It offers marketers some very real opportunities, but it also carries some risks.

Sending an unsolicited e-mail sales message to someone is asking for trouble. Not many people like the paper junk mail they receive at home and in the office; they tend to hate unsolicited e-mail. Regular users of the Internet, and increasingly the popular press, describe unsolicited e-mail as spam and sending such e-mail as spamming.

It is possible to rent and use mailing lists for e-mail in much the same way you may have done for printed mailers. Only you can decide if the potential business this might generate is worth the almost certain backlash from angry recipients.

A better way of dealing with e-mail as a marketing tool is to invite people who visit your Web site to ask for e-mail news. For example, you could offer to send people an occasional e-mail newsletter, which will keep them updated about new products, prices, or promotions. A simple form on a page on your Web site would allow readers to register to receive the news and the same page should assure people that you will keep their identities and addresses private.

3. Costs

Nothing is free and marketing your gift basket business on the Internet is no exception to that rule.

The good news is that the cost of Internet tools are continuing to fall. Setting up a simple Web site such as the brochure-type site should not cost more than $500 and the monthly running cost (space rental from an ISP) is likely to be in the $20 to $30 range.

Build something fancier and your costs will inevitably be higher. A Web site that allows credit card orders to be placed and cleared while the buyer is online may cost several thousand dollars to prepare and your ISP may charge in the range of $100 a month for the service.

Someone is going to have to attend to the Web site and this is a cost. For the simplest, brochure-type site, the cost of maintenance will be negligible. Step up to a site that accepts orders or allows visitor inquiries and you will need to have someone paying daily attention to the communications generated by the site.

4. Location, location

Companies that research Internet statistics said there were more than 800,000 Web pages on the Internet in late 1999. They also said that the search facilities most users employ to find information on the Internet, index less than 15% of those pages. So how can you be sure anyone will ever visit your Web site?

You may consider creating a neutral Web page that acts as a starting point for someone interested in the gift industry, and link your Web site (as well as other sites that would be of interest to surfers) to this site. Many trade associations, tourist promotion boards, and similar bodies may already offer such a jumping-off point to which you can have your Web site added, often at no cost.

Don't forget to publicize your Web site on your print brochure, business card, direct mail piece, and invoices.

5. Getting started

There are plenty of people out there selling Internet Snake Oil! Check with friends, neighbors, and business associates to get pointers to reliable help. Don't overlook local colleges and high schools; both may have teacher-led programs that can help you get a Web site launched inexpensively. In many cities the main library now has Internet resources and staff who can help you.

Start small and start cautiously. You will still be in business tomorrow even if you don't have a Web site with all the bells and whistles today. And almost every aspect of doing business on the Internet will be less expensive tomorrow.

l. Seasonal Advertising

Depending on the type of business you seek, you may want to divide your advertising and marketing dollars to cover the various seasons of gift giving. In addition to recurring business from birthdays, anniversaries, new babies, weddings, retirements, and get-well gifts, the following are the standard seasons for a typical gift packaging company:

- Valentine's Day
- Easter
- Mother's Day
- Father's Day
- Thanksgiving
- Hanukkah
- Christmas
- New Year's Day

Businesses located in certain areas may also want to promote the following gift giving occasions:

- Chinese New Year or other major ethnic celebrations or national days
- Cruise ship bon voyage gifts or gifts for meetings and conventions

For a typical gift packaging company in North America, the highest volume of business is done during the December holiday period. It is estimated that this season accounts for more than 40% of annual gross sales. A larger portion of your advertising budget should be allocated at this time. Have your program in place by mid-September.

Most publications have special features and sections for gift business advertisers and you may also want to consider having your brochure included as an insert. It is also a good time to do another direct mailing and possibly a telemarketing promotion.

m. Special Promotions

An excellent way of promoting your business and of expanding your customer base is to organize or become involved with special events and promotions. Sometimes involvement costs little or no more than your time and a possible donation of a gift package. Following are a few ideas you may want to follow through with for special promotions.

1. Open house/grand opening

Depending on the size of your facility, you may want to have a series of wine and cheese parties to promote the opening of your new business. When my company moved into a new office building, we invited all the other tenants for an open house when our holiday gift brochure was ready. The business that came from that promotion more than paid for the cost of the party and for the printing and design of the brochure.

2. Small giveaways

Small giveaways with your company name and phone number fall under the category of advertising specialty items and as your business grows, it is a natural area for you to expand into. The giveaway item need not be expensive, but it should be useful and have your company name and phone number prominently printed on it. Over the years my company has given away pads of notepaper, portfolios, pens, mini address books, clothing, aprons, and other desk items.

3. Fairs and craft shows

Almost every community has craft shows or public fairs and events where you can rent booth space and promote your product, and in some cases sell directly to the consumer. Some of these shows tend to be expensive so make sure that it is a well-publicized event and has been successful for a number of years before committing yourself. (See the Appendix for a list of fairs and craft shows throughout North America.)

4. Trade shows

Generally trade shows are aimed toward a specific market. I take a booth at an annual cruise industry trade show to promote my Alaska cruise gift business. Again, make sure that the return will warrant the cost. (See the Appendix for a list of fairs and trade shows throughout North America.)

5. Displays

Place displays in office lobbies or other high-traffic public buildings. During the December holiday season some office buildings or government buildings will allow artists and craftspeople to set up displays or booths to promote their work. You might not be allowed to sell products on the premises, but it can be an effective way to promote your business.

6. Donations

Donate gifts and baskets for auctions and charitable events. You may find yourself overwhelmed by requests for donations of gift baskets during the year, and it is best to choose a couple of very high-profile events to become involved with and commit to them on an annual basis.

7. Community events and organizations

I once volunteered to organize the food exhibitors at a charitable fundraising international wine festival. In return for my efforts I was allowed to have a booth promoting my business at the event. I held my own prize draw during the evening and came away with hundreds of new customers.

n. Measuring Advertising Effectiveness

Get into the habit of asking new clients how they heard about your company. Note whether it was word-of-mouth, Yellow Pages, direct mail, your Web site or printed advertising. After a few months you should have a good feel for what type of advertising is working for you. It can take up to six months for an advertising program to show any visible return, so don't expect miracles overnight.

Make up an advertising and promotions expense breakdown and compare the costs with the benefits in sales. Sample 13 shows an example of such a breakdown for both a studio/office and a home-based business.

SAMPLE 13
ADVERTISING AND PROMOTIONS EXPENSE BREAKDOWN

* Studio/office:	Monthly	Quarterly	Annually
Yellow pages (2" x 2" ad)	$150	$450	$1,800
Opening promo and yearly			1,250
Print advertising (10x)	250	625	2,500
Direct mail (4x)		1,000	4,000
TOTAL	$400	$2,075	$9,550

*Note: Budget is based on spending from 3% to 5% of gross projected sales ($250,000) on advertising.

*Home-based:	Monthly	Quarterly	Annually
Yellow Pages (¾ ad)		$48	$570
Opening promo and yearly			540
Print advertising (December)			250
Direct mail (2x)			1,890
TOTAL		$48	$3,250

*Note: Budget is based on spending from 3% to 5% of gross projected sales ($65,000) on advertising.

By advertising one specific product, you can measure the return by the number of phone calls you receive regarding the product and the number of sales that you make. A direct-mail program should give you more of an immediate indication whether the piece is working for you or not. When my company actively went after the cruise ship gift business in my community, we sent out our first professionally designed, full-color photographic brochure. The response was immediate and overwhelming.

When we asked our customers why they had ordered from us rather than one of the many other companies providing the same service, they said the piece was too beautiful to ignore. The repeat business comes from giving excellent service and a quality product.

Chapter 9
SALES AND MARKETING

a. Personal Contacts

One of the advantages of a gift basket business is that almost everyone you know and meet could be a long-term, repeat customer. Even in casual social situations, the conversations usually come around to what people do for a living, and without being too obvious, you can make new customers just about anywhere.

Be able to explain what you do and what your business involves clearly and succinctly in 30 seconds. For example, you might say something like this: "I'm busy running a small, successful gift basket business. We supply gift baskets with a variety of styles and themes for any occasion. We're proud of our broad base of customers — everyone from major corporations to individual purchasers. If you're ever interested, I'd be pleased to show you our samples!"

When someone expresses interest in your company, give a business card (you should have a supply of business cards with you at all times) and offer to send a company brochure or invite them to visit your showroom. A satisfied customer can pass your name along to several people, who in turn can pass your name on to more people, and so on.

Word-of-mouth advertising is the most cost effective way of promoting your business. Most successful gift basket company owners are highly active and social people and are involved with many organizations in their community. It is feasible to make new business contacts and find potential customers at your place of worship, school parent association meetings, political meetings, health club or country club, hair salon, community center, card club, alumni association, or any other place where you would meet people on a regular basis. Almost everyone you meet will be in need of a gift at sometime or another, so make sure that your friends and acquaintances are aware of what you do for a living.

b. Networking

Networking is the exchange of information or services among individuals, groups, or institutions. Networking can be as simple as having lunch with a friend who is well connected in the business community who may give you names of a few potential customers to contact, to a more formal, organized networking group.

There are a number of these organizations active in North America that you may want to consider getting involved with. I belong to a networking organization called BRE, which stands for Business Referral Exchange. The group I belong to can have up to 30 members with only one member per business type allowed. Members include a lawyer, accountant, investment counselor, public relations expert, graphic designer, real estate agent, travel agent, and salespeople representing insurance, printing, foreign exchange, and advertising companies to name just a few. My company is the only gift business represented in my group. For a nominal monthly fee we meet once a week for an hour and a half, exchange business cards and leads, and listen to two of the members give ten-minute presentations about their business and services. BRE was founded on the premise that a business person should never have to make a cold call, and that by expanding your network of business contacts, qualified leads will come your way. Belonging to this type of organization has generated good business for my company and if you do not have a networking organization already in place in your community, you may want to consider starting one.

Selling to corporations can be some of your most profitable business. Most businesses need gifts on a regular basis, not just during the holiday season. Many companies recognize employee anniversaries, birthdays, promotions, retirements, thank-yous, out-of-town visitors, and guest speakers during the year. Most businesses do not have the time or personnel to devote to shopping. Forming a good relationship with a gift company can solve all of their gift-giving dilemmas.

c. Memberships

There are numerous organizations in every community that you should consider joining and becoming actively involved with. Taking a membership in a business organization costs money and involves time, so find those that provide the best networking opportunities and generate the most business. Following are a few examples of organizations you may want to consider as well as an estimate of what your annual dues might be.

1. Tourism, convention, or visitors' bureau

If you live in a community that is a tourist destination or has the hotels and meeting facilities for conventions, a membership in this type of organization could be very important to your business. Attending the meetings and functions will give you an opportunity to meet people involved with the tourism and hospitality industry who are all potential buyers of your services.

Most tourism organizations also publish a confidential list of upcoming conventions and a contact name with an address and telephone number. If you make a point of getting to know the people within the tourism organization, they can be a good source of leads and are usually very loyal to members who have a proven track record of providing good product and service. Annual dues are $200 to $400.

2. Board of Trade or Chamber of Commerce

Most members of this type of organization are the leaders of industry and business owners in a community. Meetings are usually held at breakfast or lunch and feature a guest speaker. My local Board of Trade offers a once-a-month function called Business after Business. This function takes place in a different hotel ballroom or other large venue every month and members can take a table to display their products and services for a fee.

The general public is invited to attend and it gives the companies involved a chance to meet face-to-face with potential customers for two hours. I have always come away with more than enough business to justify the time and expense involved. Annual dues are $300 to $600.

3. Meeting Professionals International

Meeting Professionals International (MPI) is an international organization of meeting planners and affiliated suppliers; most chapters are in the United States and Canada. As a gift company you would join as a supplier. Local chapters have monthly meetings and a membership in this type of organization offers excellent potential for sales to members who are planning meetings and conventions in your area, as well as to other supplier members. Annual dues are $350.

4. *International Special Events Society*

International Special Events Society (ISES) attracts members in the event industry such as special event planners, caterers, decorating companies, tent rental companies, entertainment companies, and party equipment rental companies. There are excellent opportunities for leads and business with this organization. Annual dues are $295.

Depending on the type of business you are going after, there are many other types of organizations that you might decide to join. If you are actively going after travel business, you could join one of the many organizations for travel agents as an affiliate or supplier member. If you think that people involved with the hotel industry may offer you the most potential business, then you might consider joining the Hotel Sales and Marketing Association.

These types of organizations are very specific, so it is probably wise to stick with one or two memberships to start that offer a more varied membership base. It costs money to take a membership in any organization, not only in annual dues, but in the cost of the monthly meetings or special functions. Belonging to an organization is a commitment of your time as well as money, so be prepared to attend the meetings and functions if you want your membership to pay for itself in future business. Most organizations and associations are listed in the Yellow Pages and notices of meetings are usually listed once a week in the business section of the newspaper. One of the other advantages of taking a membership in a large organization is that they will then provide you with a complete membership roster, which will help in starting your potential customer data base and mailing list.

d. Top Down Marketing

Most small business owners promote their companies using bottom up marketing. An example of bottom up marketing is when you send your company brochure in the mail to potential clients, follow up with a phone call, and wait for the orders to come in. A more positive approach is for you to create a need for the customer to use your products and services. This is called top down marketing. Following are some examples of ways that you can promote your company using top down marketing.

1. New product launches and company promotions

Market your gift basket services to food or beverage manufacturers, food marketing boards, and other businesses. Offer to promote their products in your baskets and to make up baskets for their promotions. Over the years my company has worked with large liquor and wine distributors, international mineral water producers, marketing boards promoting fruit, cheese, and seafood, publishing companies promoting new cookbooks, restaurants, and many small gourmet food manufacturers. These companies did not contact me, I contacted them.

Not only has my company received actual orders and business by doing this, but we have also generated free publicity and exposure that would have been impossible to attain without working in conjunction with another company.

2. Special events

Offer to donate baskets or provide baskets to use as table centerpieces for charity events or business functions. The baskets can be given away as prizes and it is usual for you to put some type of advertising piece at each place setting as well as to be promoted as a sponsor of the event.

This type of marketing can give your business excellent exposure and will generate sales if you choose the events that you want to become involved with carefully as well as the time of year that the event occurs.

3. Noncompeting businesses

During the December holiday selling period (October through December), get involved with other companies to promote their products within your gift baskets. There are many gourmet specialty food and wine and liquor retailers, distributors, and manufacturers who do not have the time or inclination to promote their products in gift baskets. You should contact this type of company in the summer and offer to put together a gift basket program for them. They may decide to buy the made-up baskets from you to sell in their store or have your baskets on display and take the orders for you. The remuneration that you work out depends on the type of operation they have and if you are purchasing products from them to include in the baskets.

e. Selling Your Product and Services

At this point you should have the following selling tools which enable you to make sales presentations in person or over the phone and to take orders:

(a) Professionally designed sales brochure, product list, and price list

(b) Business cards and stationery

(c) Gift tags, enclosure card, and gift labels

(d) Fax-back order form

(e) Samples of all the gift packages, containers, and products

(f) Web site

You can use all of these items to sell at every opportunity.

1. Making the sale by telephone

When you are selling from your place of business over the telephone, always follow these steps:

(a) Answer your business phone in a professional manner: "Good morning, ABC Gift Baskets, this is Mary speaking."

(b) If the customer is not ordering one of your standard baskets, be prepared to ask a lot of questions.

(c) Determine the type of basket the customer is looking for and the budget.

(d) Be sure to advise customers if there are any additional delivery charges or applicable taxes.

(e) If the customer can't make a decision, offer to fax several different options.

(f) When the customer places the order, have a binder with an order form ready to take all the pertinent information. Use this binder to add customers and recipients into the data base. Be sure to thank the customer for the order.

(g) If the customer is paying by credit card over the phone, fax a confirmation of the order and ask that it be signed and faxed back to you.

(h) When the order is complete and the basket has been picked up for delivery, fax back the customer a copy of the credit card receipt or a copy of the invoice if he or she is paying by check. Send the originals in the mail. Send another sales brochure at this time. Thank the customer for the order.

(i) If you satisfy customers with your product and service, the next time they order they will probably be inclined to just send the order to you by fax, thus saving both of you the time spent on the phone.

2. Making a sales presentation

If you are seeing customers at their place of business, always phone the day or morning before the appointment to confirm the time and to make sure that it is convenient for you to see them. Be on time, even a few minutes early. Dress professionally.

If the customer is coming to your showroom or office, treat him or her like a guest in your home. Take any coats or wraps and hang them up. Offer coffee or some type of cold drink. Take a few minutes to make a social conversation. Offer a seat and exchange business cards. Give customers a bit of time to relax before you start to sell.

Ask questions, listen to the customer, and make eye contact. Asking questions and listening to customers enables you to determine exactly what their needs are, and gives you additional ideas of ways to serve them in order to make the sale.

Know your product and be able to clearly explain what the benefits of your gift packages and services are. Offer to leave a sample with your customer to be picked up by you at a specified time. When the customer places an order, offer to send a confirmation in writing, and do it before the end of the next business day. Thank him or her for the order verbally and in writing. Always thank customers for either taking the time to visit you or for letting you call on them.

Know when to wind things up. Do not waste the customer's time.

f. The Importance of Service

How you treat your customers and the quality of service you provide is what will make them come back to you again, and it is also what brings you new customers by referral. Building a strong, satisfied customer base is the key to the success of your new venture. Repeat business and word-of-mouth advertising is essential to the profitability of your company. Providing an excellent product at a reasonable price is not enough to move ahead of your competition. You must also provide excellent service and go that extra mile to make sure your customers are satisfied. Employ the following tips:

(a) Remember that the customer is always right. Never argue with a customer.

(b) If you tell a customer that you will do something in a certain time frame, do it.

(c) If the customer asks you a question that you cannot answer, tell the truth and offer to find the information quickly.

(d) If you lose an order to another company, do not complain or ask the customer who they ordered from and why. Have a positive attitude and thank the customer for his or her time and consideration. Say that you look forward to doing business with him or her some time in the future.

(e) If a customer places an order with a competitor, do not offer to undercut the competition's price; that makes you look unprofessional and isn't worth it to your profit margin.

(f) If there is a problem with an order, rectify the problem quickly and without argument.

(g) If an item in a basket or the type of container must be substituted, always make the customer aware before the order is processed.

(h) Be friendly, polite, professional, and positive. It isn't that difficult because the gift business is a happy business. It is your job to make the customer happy.

Chapter 10
EMPLOYEES AND PERSONNEL

a. Being a Sole Owner/Operator

In the start-up phase and early stages of your new business, it is unlikely that you will be in a financial position to hire employees. Be prepared to devote some long hours to your business and to be responsible for all aspects of running your own company. The sole owner/operator must wear many hats and be responsible for looking after all of the following areas of the gift packaging company:

(a) Physically making up the gift packages

(b) Overseeing the design and manufacturing of all sales and collateral materials

(c) Marketing and promoting the product and service

(d) Purchasing equipment, supplies, and inventory

(e) Processing orders by phone or fax and sending out quotations

(f) Looking after the delivery/shipping of the products

(g) Managing the office

(h Accounting/bookkeeping, receivable and payable

(i) Banking

(j) Filing and keeping all the records and materials organized

Managing your time is the key to being successful. Although it may be necessary to work in the evenings and on weekends, especially in the early stages of your business, try to get into the habit of organizing your schedule for regular office hours during the week.

Divide each of the five working days into quarters and schedule tasks and duties for each. For example:

- 8:00 a.m. to 10:00 a.m. — outside deliveries, pickups, banking, mailing sales kit, etc.

- 10:00 a.m. to 12:00 noon — make sales phone calls, answer faxes, correspondence.

- 12:00 noon to 1:00 p.m. — lunch or personal errands.

- 1:00 p.m. to 3:00 p.m. — take inventory, make up baskets, order supplies and stocks.

- 3:00 p.m. to 5:00 p.m. — write checks, type invoices, bookkeeping, filing, and office duties.

Your personal life will dictate to some extent the best way to organize your time, but if you get into the habit of scheduling your time and stick with it, you will be surprised how much can be accomplished by one person in a regular work week. I know of many small gift basket company owners who have no desire to expand their business to the point where it is necessary to bring in additional help and to hire employees. That is fine if you are satisfied with a certain amount of business and income and are not interested in seeing your company expand and grow. But there is only so much business one person can handle, and if you do decide that you want to expand your business, it will be necessary to hire additional help.

b. Casual Labor and Seasonal Helpers

Even if you decide to run your business alone, there will be times during the year when the volume of orders makes it physically impossible to operate effectively by yourself. The majority of your December holiday business will take place the two weeks prior to December 25, and if you have marketed your services properly, you should have more than enough orders to warrant bringing in outside help.

University students are a good source of workers at this time of year as they are usually on their winter break. Contact the student employment office of your local college or university in the late fall to post your notice of employment wanted. As well, many full-time homemakers who are not interested in regular employment are willing to work at this time to earn extra money for holiday expenses or upcoming vacations expenses.

I have always found this type of help simply by telling friends or acquaintances that I am looking for someone. You could also spread the word by posting a notice in your gym, place of worship, or social club.

The laws vary by state, province, or country as to the maximum amount a person can earn as a casual laborer before the employer must register him or her as an employee and deduct taxes. The minimum wage laws also vary, and you should find out what the legal requirements are in your area before hiring. Depending on the duties performed, this type of helper would earn from $6 to $8 per hour. Normally you would hire this type of employee to help assemble baskets, take orders, answer phones, make deliveries (compensate employees who make deliveries for gas and mileage, over and above their hourly pay), and do general office clean-up.

If you are lucky enough to find someone with creative and artistic abilities, you may want to train him or her to assemble gift package orders. The way your gift packages look is a reflection of your company, so it is necessary to oversee and train an employee to take on this responsibility and to make sure that the high standard of quality is maintained.

c. Hiring an Assistant

As your business grows and prospers, you will want to hire either a full-time or part-time assistant. Choose this person carefully, as you will spend a lot of time together and he or she will reflect your company. This person must be compatible with you and be capable of running your business when you are away.

Hire someone who is personable, self-motivated, organized, a quick learner, and a team player. These traits are more important than any previous gift packaging experience. If the person has the above attributes, you can teach him or her anything he or she does not already know. This person can be trained to take on management duties such as inventory control and ordering of supplies, which will free up some of your time and allow you to concentrate on selling and marketing your services. Hire someone who is creative and able to get along well with your suppliers and your customers. Depending on the responsibilities of the position, compensation should be from $8 to $12 per hour.

d. Office Manager/ Bookkeeper

Depending on the size of your business and the sales volume, this position can be either part-time or full-time. When you reach the point of needing this type of employee, it is probably wise to first bring someone in on a part-time basis and increase the hours as the business warrants. Maintaining accurate books and records is essential to your business and as your company becomes more successful, the more time these tasks will take. My company office manager/bookkeeper is in charge of all accounts payable and receivable, payroll, banking, regular filing of local and federal taxes, employee expense accounts, updating customer and supplier data base, entering inventory into the data base, maintaining company insurance, business licenses, and corporate records, monthly financial statements, office supplies and stationery, office equipment supplies and maintenance, postage and mailing, and year-end inventory and tax preparation.

The office manager/bookkeeper should also be familiar with all aspects of the business and be able to comfortably answer phones and deal with customers if necessary. If you only need help of this nature on a part-time basis, one or two days a week, it may be possible to hire someone who does this type of work for several different companies. This type of person will then work for you under contract and bill you for their services once or twice a month. It is not necessary for you to put them on your payroll. Depending on their experience and responsibilities, expect to pay between $12 to $15 per hour for this type of employee.

e. Hiring and Keeping Good Employees

Finding and hiring the right employees for your business is not an easy task. Keeping good employees after you have hired and trained them is even more difficult, but one that is essential to the continued growth and success of your company. One of the most difficult decisions a small business owner will have to make is knowing when it is time to hire personnel.

Many small business owners are reticent about hiring because they have a fear of bringing someone they do not know into their organization who may be dishonest or end up becoming competition. Letting these fears hold you back from hiring employees will also prevent you from attaining growth and increased profitability.

Many small businesses fail or never move to higher income and profit levels because the owner is not willing to expand the business by hiring employees. Do not waste all the time, effort, and money that you have spent in starting your business by not knowing when it is time to expand and hire. For a gift basket business to be successful, there must be someone to handle the creative side of the company as well as the business side. When the volume of business reaches a level that you, as sole owner, are unable to handle, it is time to hire or the whole business will stagnate.

Know what you expect of an employee before you start looking. Before hiring anyone, you should have done the following:

(a) Create a job description which includes —

- Job title

- Responsibilities

- Duties

- Expected hours and work days

- When vacations can and cannot be taken

- Paid holidays

- Remuneration

(b) Outline job specifications and qualifications —

- Education

- Previous experience

- Special skills (computer and keyboard skills, etc.)

- Special requirements (calligraphy, driver's license, etc.)

1. Common sense guidelines to hiring employees

(a) Do not hire friends or relatives as employees

This type of arrangement rarely works out and it is usually too difficult for most friends or relatives to be treated as employees and to treat you as an employer. If a friend or relative does not work out and you must let him or her go, you not only lose an employee, but you risk losing a personal relationship.

(b) Ask for recommendations

Ask business associates whose judgment you respect if they can recommend potential employees. Personal references can often provide the most suitable people.

(c) Contact job placement departments

Recruit potential employees by using the job placement departments at schools, colleges, universities, and community centers.

(d) Advertise

Advertising in newspaper or trade publications can be effective, but it can also be expensive and generate many more resumes than you have time to process. When writing a classified ad, be very specific about what your requirements are, the educational and work background you are looking for, and what the hours and remuneration will be.

(e) Use job application forms

Purchase job application forms from your local stationery store and have each potential job applicant fill one out. Make sure you have a complete job history, educational background, and references from each applicant. Make a short list of the most qualified people and arrange for personal interviews.

(f) Check references

If you are serious about hiring someone after an interview, make sure you check his or her references to verify employment history.

2. Common sense guidelines to keeping good employees

(a) Communication

Have an open-door policy with all your employees. Build an atmosphere in which your employees feel free to speak up and know they will be listened to. Schedule an hour each week devoted to sitting down with your staff, having a cup of coffee, and getting grievances or problems out in the open. This is also a great time to have brainstorming sessions and come up with creative ways to market your products and services. Make your employees feel that they are really part of the team and important to the success of your business.

(b) Consistency

Set standards and insist that they be met. If you can force yourself to be consistent, you will make it easy for employees to work for you, even if your standards are high. Have your standards in writing in the form of a personnel manual. Make sure that all new employees read and understand this manual at the time they are hired. If employees know what to expect, you will eliminate any future misunderstandings. If you want to curb, for example, personal phone calls, absenteeism, smoking on the work site, improper dress, gum chewing, etc. make your rules known in the hiring process. Your employees will give you what your actions say you want.

(c) Congratulations

Your employees must have pride in what they do if their work is to be good. Your product and service is the source of your employees' pride, but it is not enough just to have a good product. Your employees must know it is good and must feel that they have contributed to it. Praise your staff for a job well done and let them know when you receive written or verbal praise about them or your product and services from your customers.

(d) Compensation

Pay your employees fairly and according to what the job market in your area requires. Give them increases once they have proven themselves. One well-paid, well-trained, motivated, capable employee will serve your needs much better than three underpaid, mediocre, indifferent ones.

(e) Evaluation

Evaluate your employees. An evaluation allows you to assess the employee's performance, plan the training and development they may still require, exchange opinions, and generally build a better working relationship.

(f) Commissions and share options

If you have an employee who is hired to sell your products and services and bring in new business, it may make sense to work out a commission structure on top of a base salary or hourly wage. This type of pay structure usually motivates the employee to work hard and should increase your sales.

Most commission structures are based on attaining set sales goals, and it is therefore more appropriate for a gift company that has been in business for a few seasons to use this type of structure. A share option plan is an agreement between you and your employees in which you give your employees the right to purchase shares in your company for a certain price. The option is held open for a certain length of time. Such plans provide financial inducements for your employees to become shareholders. Granting share options can be complicated from a legal point of view, and you will need to deal with your lawyer if you are going to consider this offering.

All personnel policies operate within a legal framework. Among the many governmental regulations for employers today are the minimum wage laws, fair employment regulations, requirements for withholding income taxes, and other items from employees' pay checks for the federal, provincial, or state government, and public policy regarding safety in the workplace and equal opportunity. Before you begin hiring, check the current regulations with your local government employment department.

A successful business owner will realize that fringe benefits, health and hospital insurance, paid vacations, profit-sharing, fair wages, good working conditions, and concern for employees are all part of building a happy, dedicated, productive staff. Keeping your employees happy will help advance your business and will create an image of your gift packaging service as an excellent place to work.

Chapter 11
MAKING YOUR BUSINESS LEGAL

a. Your Legal Structure

Before you complete many of the other legal requirements mentioned later in this chapter, you will first need to decide in what legal form you will carry on your gift basket business. Your choices of the form of legal entity include a sole proprietorship, a partnership, a limited partnership, and an incorporated company. There are tax advantages and disadvantages in each of the possible business structures, and incorporation is governed by state or provincial laws. You should obtain legal and tax advice before making your final decision.

1. Sole proprietorship

As the name indicates, a sole proprietorship is when there is only one owner. This is the simplest way to carry on business and may have tax advantages for you early in the operation of the business as any losses you have may be deducted from income you may make from other sources.

Just because you are the sole owner doesn't mean to say that you could not have one or more employees, but the profits and losses from the business are all yours.

2. Partnership

If you have two or more people who will be owners of the business, then you can create a partnership (if you decide not to incorporate a company, as discussed below). Partnerships can be quite complicated from a legal point of view, as many of the terms of a partnership agreement must be created by your lawyer. Partnerships have the advantage that losses might also be deducted from your other income, but have the large disadvantage that each partner is personally liable for any losses or breach of contract, even if the other partners do not pay their fair share.

If you form a partnership, you should consider how you will buy out that person's interest if he or she becomes disabled or dies. You may wish to consider obtaining life insurance on each partner which is payable to the partnership or to the remaining partners.

3. Limited partnerships

This type of partnership involves a silent partner who may contribute money to your business and receive a share of the profits, but who would not be actively involved in running the business. Limited partnerships must be set up in a special fashion, and it is unlikely that you would be able to create one without the assistance of a lawyer.

4. Incorporation

Whether you are just a one-person business or whether two or more of you will carry on business together, you can incorporate a company to carry on your business. To avoid confusion, you should note that the word "company" is often used to describe a sole proprietorship or some other type of business, and the proper legal word is "corporation," not company.

All states and provinces allow one or more persons to incorporate a business, but there are significant fees for the privilege of creating a corporation and usually subsequent annual fees to keep your corporation in good standing.

Having a corporation is the most sophisticated way of carrying on business and customers will be more impressed than if you were a sole proprietorship or partnership. Corporations offer great flexibility as you may issue shares in your corporation to your co-owners, in differing proportions, and with different rights for those shares. For example, if a relative were prepared to invest in your business but you did not want him or her to have any say in the day-to-day operations of your business, then you could create a special class of nonvoting shares for that person.

There are various tax implications — both advantages and disadvantages — to having a corporation. Some states and provinces have lower tax rates for small corporations and you can have the profits of the gift basket business taxed at a lower rate, as long as you do not pay out all of the profits to the shareholders of your corporation by way of salaries or dividends.

Corporations generally have the advantage of limited liability, which simply means that the individual shareholders would not be personally liable for debts of the corporation if the business went under. You should note that this protection of limited liability does not extend to negligence (e.g., if you or your co-owners cause some personal damage to someone during the course of the business, then you or your co-owners, and possibly your company, could all be sued for negligence). The limited liability of a corporation only extends to its debts.

Unfortunately, sophisticated lenders or grantors of credit, such as banks and major suppliers, often want the individual shareholders to guarantee the corporation's debts, thereby taking away the advantage of limited liability.

Although it is certainly possible to incorporate a business yourself, you should consider using the services of a lawyer. The paperwork for an incorporation itself is not usually very difficult, but the advice that the lawyer can provide both before and after incorporation can be invaluable. If you do decide to incorporate, you must rigorously carry out all of the requirements set out, including what to do after incorporation and what to do each year in order to keep your corporation in good standing (i.e., not being canceled by the state or province because of your failure to file any required annual documents).

Remember that there will be continuing costs relating to maintaining your corporation including annual filing fees, as noted above, but also the additional cost of preparing a separate income tax return for your corporation.

As with partnerships, if there is to be more than one owner in the corporation, you should consider obtaining life and disability insurance on the other shareholders so that a shareholder can be bought out with the insurance if he or she dies or becomes disabled.

b. Using the Services of Professionals

No one starting a new business wants to spend more money than he or she has to, but the time will come when your new business needs professional advice on matters of law or accounting.

Accounting and law are highly specialized areas, and each is subject to constant change. It is difficult for the small business person to keep up with these changes and still run a profitable business.

Although professional advice is expensive, it is often necessary to avoid costly mistakes. If you are unsure of legalities that affect your business or you are confused about proper accounting procedures, you should use the services of a qualified accountant and lawyer.

For example, before deciding on whether to incorporate, seek the advice of a professional tax accountant who can advise you on whether it is best for you to incorporate at the beginning, or whether it is better to delay that decision until the size of the business increases. After you have talked to the tax accountant, engage a lawyer if you need one.

Any lawyer or professional you engage must have good communication skills. A good lawyer should make it easy for you to ask questions and should explain things in simple terms. Of course, the fee structure is the other important consideration of hiring a lawyer or other professional. You should never hesitate to ask about the fee at the beginning and you should ask for frequent billings so that you can always keep an eye on how your legal costs are rising.

It is wise to plan for your professional services early in your business cycle to take the time to select who you want to act for your new business and to check credentials. The other option is to wait until you have a problem. This method can be perilous. If your mind is occupied with a problem, it is not always clear enough to choose an adviser wisely. If the problem is serious and you are under stress, you may even engage the wrong person entirely and spend more time and money than you need to. It is better to establish a comfortable working relationship from the beginning. You do not need to pay a king's ransom for professional services if you prepare yourself and your business properly.

c. Choosing Your Name — Legally

Choosing the right name for your business is important. In chapter 8, I discussed some issues to think about when choosing your name to make it suitable for your business and to help customers remember it. But there are legal considerations as well.

First, file and protect the name you have chosen. You can always operate your business under your proper name (e.g., Melanie's Gift Baskets), but if you choose a fictitious name (e.g., Gifts for Every Occasion), or your name implies that more than one person owns the business (e.g., Melanie and Company), most jurisdictions require that such names be registered. This is done by filing a "fictitious name statement" with county or provincial authorities.

When you register a fictitious name, it will be checked against previously filed names to ensure the name has not been taken by another business. This is for your protection too.

Many people start their businesses and do not register the name. This can be a costly mistake. You may operate for a few months or longer, all the while spending time and money to get your company name recognized and respected, then one day you receive a registered letter telling you to stop using it. Too late, you find out that the name is already used and protected by someone else. You may even be liable for damages. Once your name is on file, it cannot be used by anyone else.

It is a good idea to have two, or even three, names ready before you register. That way, if your first choice is rejected, you will have another name ready and you won't have to start all over again. A quick — though not foolproof — way to check the availability of the name is to scan your local telephone book.

In Canada, you can have a name search done through the provincial ministry that handles incorporations. This will also tell you if the name is registered out of province. This process takes about a week and there is a small fee, generally under $50.

In the United States, your city or county clerk will tell you if the name is available for use.

In some states and provinces, it is also possible to have a "trading name" for your corporation, which gives you the flexibility to change the name in the future, should the nature of your business change or become more comprehensive. If you incorporate under the name Melanie's Gift Baskets Inc., for example, you may later find the name to be a disadvantage when you have branched out into other services.

When choosing your trading name or your actual incorporated name, you should also keep in mind the advantage of having a name which is self-advertising. Although there are disadvantages to having a name like Melanie's Gift Basket Inc., which you may later want to change, in the beginning it at least tells your customers exactly what your business is. A name like Melanie's Enterprises Inc. does not describe your business, so the listing of your name in the white pages, or in any other listing where your name only is displayed, generates no publicity for you.

You will probably need to consult a lawyer if you wish to have a trading name.

d. Insurance Requirements

Always discuss your insurance needs with a professional. If you are starting your business out of your home, you will find that your standard homeowner policy is not enough to meet the needs of your business. It will not cover things such as lawsuits, damages, or accidents that may result from your business.

If you are starting your business in leased or rental space, you will also have to consider business liability insurance. An insurance professional can help set up a policy that is right for you.

Some types of insurance you may want to think about are as follows:

(a) General liability (which may or may not be covered by your lease): Covers against liability that may happen within or outside your premises, such as an employee being involved in an accident, a person falling over in your office, a gift basket containing food that turns out to be contaminated, etc.

(b) Product liability: Protects against a lawsuit by a customer or client who used your product or service and, as a result, sustained bodily injury or property damage from it.

(c) Automobile liability: Covers other people's property, other automobiles, persons in other vehicles, and persons in the insured automobile. If you are using your car for business purposes, exclusively or occasionally, it is important that you have your premium cover business use. It is possible that your current motor vehicle insurance policy has just a premium based on personal use. Problems could occur if there were an accident and it was discovered that your car was used for business purposes.

(d) Fire and theft liability: Covers against damage and loss due to fire or theft.

(e) Business interruption insurance: The indirect loss from a fire or theft can be greater than the loss itself. You will not only have the cost of carrying on the business temporarily from some other location, you will also possibly have losses because you will have lost your accounts receivables records, or other records which are essential to your business.

(f) Personal disability insurance: Covers the possibility of your being disabled for a short or long period of time. This insurance pays you a certain monthly amount if you are permanently disabled, or a portion of that amount if you are partially disabled, but capable of generating some income.

There may be other forms of insurance that you should have, and your insurance broker is the best person to discuss these with.

e. Leases and Rental Agreements

Apart from setting up the form of legal entity that you will use, the most important legal matter to be considered is the form of any lease that you may wish to enter into. If you lease space on a month-to-month basis, the terms of the written or verbal lease agreement will be much less important because if you are unhappy with anything that the landlord does, you can always give notice and find premises elsewhere. The big disadvantage is, of course, that a landlord can also give you notice, and you could certainly find your business out on the street.

A written, long-term lease has the advantage of giving you security of your whereabouts for a fixed time, but also forces the obligation on you to keep paying for that lease, whether or not your business is successful.

While it is up to you to consider the practicalities of any location that you propose to lease (see chapter 2 on location), you should probably hire a lawyer to review any proposed lease. Leases can be tedious to read, but you should not just rely on your lawyer reading it. At a very minimum, you will need to know the answers to the following questions when you and your lawyer review the proposed lease:

(a) Is it clear how much the rent is? Many leases have a fixed basic rent, but on top of that rent you are also required to pay a proportionate share of the operating costs for the building which contains your proposed premises. These operating costs, which include the property taxes, insurance, utilities, cleaning, and other costs incurred by the landlord in running that particular building, can be as much as the basic rent itself. Most landlords will be vague about the operating costs of the building (in part because they have to estimate the costs for the forthcoming year, but you should get something in writing that gives a firm estimate of what these operating costs might be).

(b) Is it clear that your type of business will be permitted in the leased premises, and is there any prohibition on having a showroom which is open to the public? The portion of the lease that refers to the type of business to be carried on in the premises should be as wide in specification as possible.

(c) What happens if, prior to the end of the term of the lease, the business is sold, moved elsewhere, or closed down? Leases generally have special provisions about your right to assign the lease or sublet part of your space in your lease to someone else, and this section should be reviewed very carefully.

(d) Is there a right of renewal? It is a common practice for a tenant to ask for a "right of renewal" provision in any lease, so that you (and not the landlord), have the option to renew the lease for a further term after the expiry of the initial term. These options to renew will have special time limits, and this section should be carefully reviewed by you and your lawyer.

(e) What are the insurance provisions? Every lease will have some kind of provision for insurance — whether you have to get your own insurance, or pay part of the landlord's insurance. (Also note the other forms of insurance that you will also need, discussed in the section above.)

Not only should you have all the insurance clauses in the proposed lease reviewed by your lawyer, you should also make sure that the whole lease is given to your insurance broker so that he or she can make certain that you have obtained all of the insurance that is required by your landlord.

f. Zoning Laws and Business Licenses

1. Zoning laws

Whether you lease premises or are home-based, check with the local authority (which may be a county, municipality, city, or even state or provincial authority) to see whether your business can be legally carried out from the proposed premises. Many apartment buildings prohibit any kind of business. In some cases, you may even be prohibited from carrying on a gift basket business from your own single family dwelling.

Normally, there are four types of zoning defined in local codes: agricultural, commercial, industrial, and residential. In most agricultural zones, home businesses can be operated with very few restrictions, and in commercial areas, the rule is generally to allow both commercial and residential activities. If you live in either of these zones, you can expect few if any problems.

Restrictions on the kind of business you can run from a home make sense. They are designed to protect neighborhoods from some of the more intrusive elements that can be a part of a business enterprise, such as odor, noise, excess traffic, and pollution. You may find other rules that severely limit your ability to operate, such as not being allowed to sell retail, employ anyone other than family members, or store inventory.

2. Licenses

You must be licensed to operate a business. It is the law. What licenses you need will vary among regions, but if you fail to obtain and pay the annual license fee, your local authorities may close down your business.

Check with city hall or your county clerk to see what the requirement is for your business. Your local Chamber of Commerce is also a source of information on permits and licenses.

If you are going to offer liquor or alcohol items in your baskets, check whether there are any special requirements or licenses needed. The laws and regulations regarding the inclusion of wine or spirits in gift packages not only vary between states and provinces, but between counties and parishes. There are still "dry" counties where the sale or consumption of alcohol is illegal.

Where I operate my business, the government has fairly strong restrictions and we are allowed to offer the inclusion of alcohol only as a service to our customers. The product cannot be marked up over the price we pay for it.

Contact your local government agency in your community regarding the laws concerning the sale of alcohol. In some states it may be possible to apply for a license to sell wine or spirits, and you may even be able to purchase the product from your distributors and take a markup. If you can include alcohol as a service only, make sure you include the time spent providing that service in the labor charge you add to your baskets.

g. Sales Taxes

In most states and provinces, you will be required to collect sales taxes on your sale of gift baskets and other items, and to remit those monies to the appropriate taxing authority. It is important to register ahead of time and understand what records you must keep and how often you must file tax returns. You will need a sales tax number if your business buys goods for resale. This regulation applies in all states and provinces that have sales tax.

You will also likely pay some sales taxes on products that you buy, and it will be important to keep a separate record of all sales taxes you pay. In some jurisdictions, you can deduct the sales taxes you pay against the taxes you collect. In some places, you may be able to obtain an exemption from sales tax on your purchases (because you are a reseller of those products), but the exemption will require you to properly register ahead of time. A failure to pay sales taxes can be a serious crime.

In the United States, contact your state tax office, describe your business, and get the right permit.

Some jurisdictions also charge taxes on services, as well as taxes on products, and you must be sure to comply with the appropriate requirements in the same fashion as you would with sales taxes. Most branches of government have booklets on the collection and remittance of sales and services taxes, which are usually available at no cost.

Canadian businesses must also collect and remit the goods and services tax (GST). Very few businesses are exempt from this tax, but if your annual revenue is less than a certain amount, you may fall under the "small trader" section. Contact your local Revenue Canada office for details.

h. Employee-Related Regulations

If you plan to have full- or part-time employees, you should make yourself aware of any laws relating to employment standards that may include a minimum hourly wage, holidays, hours of work, notice periods, etc. Even if an employee is prepared to break any of the mandatory employment rules, you should be aware that you might still be sued by this employee, or by the branch of government that looks after employee's rights, should you subsequently have to fire the employee, or have any other kind of disagreement with him or her. The branch of government that handles employee rights will probably have a free booklet that will outline your basic responsibilities as an employer.

If you have one or more employees, you may be obligated to comply with statutory deductions specified by the tax department. This may include deduction and remittance of the employee's income tax, social services taxes, unemployment insurance tax, pension, etc.

You will need to register with the appropriate tax department as an employer; they likely have available a booklet that explains your obligations. Even if you are a one-person business, you may need to comply with certain tax obligations if you pay yourself a salary or dividends.

Many areas have compulsory requirements to register for workers' compensation or some other form of regulation relating to coverage of industrial accidents. Some places even require a one-person firm to register and to pay fees. A failure to properly register may result in fines, or other costs relating to compensations if, for example, one of your employees is injured while on the job.

i. Miscellaneous Permits

You may or may not be required to comply with other permit requirements including a permit to place a sign outside your premises, fire department permits, and health department permits. You should also ask your lawyer whether any other registration or permits are required to carry on your business.

j. A Final Word

Don't be put off by all of the above information on rules and regulations! It's not as difficult as it sounds. Your main object is to make your proposed business "legal" from the beginning so that you will not have any unpleasant surprises in the future when you are busy making gift baskets — and money!

Chapter 12
BUSINESS ETHICS AND BEST PRACTICES

Ethics: the study of standards of conduct and moral judgment; moral philosophy.

Ethical: having to do with ethics or morality; of or conforming to moral standards. Conforming to the standards of a given profession.

With the fall of the domestic goddess for insider trading and the scandals involving big business and shady practices, the topic of business ethics is timely. If you look on the Internet you can find codes of conduct for every conceivable industry and profession, and almost all associations now ask new members to sign a code of ethics and post it in their place of business. What follows here is a sample of a tourism association code of ethics and one for the Institute of Management Consultants.

Tourism Member Code of Ethics

1. *Provide clean and well-maintained facilities and equipment for the enjoyment of their customers.*

2. *Provide visitors with exceptional customer service, information on other products, services, and attractions when requested, and treat all other members courteously, ethically, and professionally.*

3. *Handle all inquiries, requests, transactions, correspondence, and complaints promptly, courteously, and fairly.*

4. *Exercise truth in all promotional materials concerning facilities, services, and amenities provided and advise the public in a reasonable manner if and when unable to provide the level of services or facilities as advertised.*

5. *Provide customers with complete details on prices, cancellation polices and services at time of purchase and advise of changes in services, products, or costs if and when they occur.*

6. *Provide all customers with a fair exchange on their foreign currency.*

7. *Promote responsible and sustainable use of our environmental resource base when providing services and products to customers.*

8. *Abide by all applicable federal, state, provincial, and municipal laws.*

Management Consultants Code of Ethics

1. *We will serve our clients with integrity, competence, and objectivity.*

2. *We will keep client information and records of client engagements confidential and will use proprietary client information only with the client's permission.*

3. *We will not take advantage of confidential client information for ourselves or our firms.*

4. *We will not allow conflicts of interest which provide a competitive advantage to one client through our use of confidential information from another client who is a direct competitor without that competitor's permission.*

5. *We will accept only engagements for which we are qualified by our experience and competence.*

6. *We will assign staff to client engagements in accord with their experience, knowledge, and expertise.*

7. *We will immediately acknowledge any influences on our objectivity to our clients and will offer to withdraw from a consulting engagement when our objectivity or integrity may be impaired.*

8. *We will agree independently and in advance on the basis for our fees and expenses and will charge fees and expenses that are reasonable, legitimate, and commensurate with the services we deliver and the responsibility we accept.*

9. *We will disclose to our clients in advance any fees or commissions that we will receive for equipment, supplies, or services we recommend to our clients.*

10. *We will respect the intellectual property rights of our clients, other consulting firms, and sole practitioners and will not use proprietary information or methodologies without permission.*

11. *We will not advertise our services in a deceptive manner and will not misrepresent our profession.*

The following list details six prime scenarios of ethical breaches that frequently take place throughout the service industry:

1. A supplier contacts a client and says, "Tell me what 'x' company charged you, and I'll charge you less."

2. Giving a kickback in order to secure business.

3. Suppliers who bypass their client and go directly to the end user to solicit business.

4. Negative selling (i.e., speaking poorly of your competitors instead of promoting your own positive attributes).

5. Prospective clients faxing one company's bid to another to try to secure another company who can do the work for less.

6. Consistently finding faults/making up problems that occurred with an order to get a discount.

a. Good Business Ethics Make Good Business Sense

The following are a few dos and don'ts for starting up and conducting your gift basket business in an ethical and professional manner.

• As you do your market research, look at the Web sites of your competition, which is the fastest and most complete way of seeing what is happening in the gift basket marketplace. You might also consider ordering a basket or two from your closest competition to see how timely the delivery was and to check the quality of the product and the service. Do not contact a competitor and pretend to be a potential supplier or corporate customer. In the end they will find out that you have been un-truthful, and the information you gathered will not be worth the damage to your reputation. If you are afraid of being up front with a competitor in your area, you can always visit some in an area far enough away that they won't view you as a potential threat. Be honest with them, and chances are they will take some time to give you advice or point you in the right direction. I send lots of business to other gift basket companies when we are too busy to take on more work or a customer has asked for something that is not our specialty.

- Don't copy the names, ingredients, and style of baskets from another company. If you can't come up with your own unique containers, ingredients, and basket names, this is not the business for you and you should consider investing your time in something less creative.

- Don't fall into the trap of letting a customer try to make you come down in price by telling you that another company is willing to sell to them for less. Price your baskets fairly and be prepared to give volume discounts on large orders, but don't sell yourself short. All the companies that I know of who tried to win business away from a competitor by underselling the product are no longer in business.

- Don't be willing to do anything to get an order. I once had a competitor walk into the office of a customer and pretend that a sample that came was from us and that the one the customer wanted to order was actually from the competitor's company. Of course the client found out who the sample actually came from and never did business with that company again. This same gift company owner pulled a few similar stunts over the few years that she was in business. Needless to say, that gift company is no longer around.

- Think about environmental impact when designing your gift packages. Try to use as much natural, biodegradable, and recycled product as possible. We do many large orders of hundreds of packages at a time into hotels and always try to steer our customers to a tote-bag container or something that is going to have the least impact on the environment.

- Consider what charities and not-for-profit organizations you may want to support. You will be asked over and over for donations so it is important that you make note of a few. It will be easier for you to turn some charities and organizations down when you can honestly say that you do support several but can't support them all.

- Look for products from suppliers who also support charities, or give a percentage of profits to charity. There are also suppliers who plant trees, and support world wide educational, hunger, and disease programs each time an order with their company is placed.

- Find out all the tax laws pertaining to your business and follow them. Each state and province taxes goods and services differently, and it is up to you to know what the regulations are. Occasionally, I have clients tell me that some unscrupulous gift companies have told them they are not required to pay certain taxes, when in fact there are taxes that need to be paid by the customer and remitted to the government. This can become a dilemma, as you don't want to lose a sale. Your only choice is to discount the product at the taxable amount. This way, you will still have to pay the tax or you can make a decision that customers who are not willing to follow the law are not worth doing business with.

- Sometimes companies who will mark up your baskets and re-sell them to an end user might contact you. These companies might be hotel conference departments or destination management companies who are dealing with visitors who want to purchase gifts and don't have the time or the inclination to deal directly with the gift supplier. This is not an uncommon practice, and the amount that they mark up your baskets could be from 10% to as much as 40%. I try to give this type of customer a discount so that the marked-up price won't be too high for the perceived value of the basket. Other times you may be asked to pay a 10% to 15% fee to the company that sent you the business. Some people think of this as a kickback, which has a rather negative connotation. Others would consider it a commission or a finders fee and feel that it is a legitimate part of doing business. The main issue is that any money paid by you in this situation is paid to a company and not to an individual.

- Don't do anything that might keep you awake at night.

Chapter 13
ACCOUNTING, RECORD KEEPING, AND TAXES

The typical gift basket company owner is usually a highly artistic individual who prefers to focus on the creative side of the business. Record keeping, accounting, and tax concerns are often seen as unpleasant distractions from the main business of designing and selling baskets. But remember, you have started a business, not a hobby, and keeping accurate books and records is essential to your long-term success and profitability. Making sure you get all the tax deductions you are entitled to is just common sense.

Being organized and having a good bookkeeping system makes the job less unpleasant. Keeping your books current and accurate means you always have financial information immediately accessible.

You must keep up-to-date accounts because the tax department requires that you supply them with certain information and payments on a regular basis, and failing to file either federal or local government taxes can result in your company being fined.

Knowing your exact financial position at all times also helps you determine your profitability and helps you make business decisions regarding expenses, hiring employees, borrowing money, or expanding your operation. If your company is very small or operates on a seasonal basis, a simple manual accounting system is probably adequate, and the necessary information and materials you will need are available at any business stationery store.

a. Accounting and Computers

Not so long ago it would have been financially unfeasible for a small gift basket operation to consider having a computerized accounting system. In the past, these systems were very expensive and too complex for most people to understand and operate.

Since the advent of inexpensive personal computers and software, small computerized accounting systems are now affordable. Once you get over the initial hurdle of learning how to operate the system, it will save you considerable time and money. I found the prospect of learning to keep company books intimidating. I hired a professional who was familiar with the accounting software my company purchased and I learned how to use the system over a two-day period.

You can do the same if you are unsure of computers and software. Hire a professional to set up the system and teach you how to operate it. My company has grown to the point where I no longer do the bookkeeping myself, but I would be able to if necessary. Being completely familiar with the accounting program allows me to access information at any time.

There are many accounting software packages that can handle your needs. Before you purchase one, do some research and make sure the program is going to work for you. If you purchase a new computer when starting up your business, that is the time to investigate accounting software packages. If you already have a computer it will be necessary to purchase one compatible with your current equipment. CA-Simply Accounting is an excellent software package. Client services information is provided for North American users of the package:

Canada
Computer Associates International Inc.
4th Floor, 1770 Burrard Street
Vancouver, B.C. V6J 3G7
Telephone: (604) 733-2343
Fax: (604) 733-4129

United States
Computer Associates International Inc.
1 Computer Associates Plaza
Islandia, NY 11788-7000
Telephone: (800) 225-5224
Fax: (516) 342-6864

b. Bookkeeping

In the early stages of business, you may do most of the bookkeeping yourself. Hire someone to help you set up a system and teach it to you. This person may then be called upon to help you occasionally if your other work has taken precedence over keeping the books current. When your business has grown to the extent that you cannot handle the bookkeeping and office duties, hire a part-time bookkeeper to take over the job and increase his or her hours as the business warrants.

Get an accountant to handle the more complicated accounting functions and tax matters. If you keep accurate books, you should be able to give a hard copy and a computer disk to your accountants at year end, and they will then prepare your year-end financial statements and tax returns.

Organize your time so that you are always up-to-date with your record-keeping. It is essential to have current data regarding your business if you are going to make timely and wise decisions. If it looks like you are going to fall drastically behind in your accounting, hire someone to come in and get the books current. It is a healthy sign if you are so busy making sales that you don't have the time to do bookkeeping, and you should not hesitate to hire someone to help you out in one area or the other.

See Sample 14 for an example of a balance sheet for a studio/office operation.

c. Sales and Accounts Receivable

The one area of accounting that should actually be enjoyable is keeping records of the sales that you make. Sales generally fall under one of the following three categories: cash, credit card, and invoiced.

1. Cash sales

Purchase a book of blank invoice forms in triplicate. You can customize these forms with your company name by using a sticker or a rubber stamp. Write in the name, address, and telephone number of the customer (important for your records and for future direct mailing), date of the transaction, description of the product sold, price charged, any applicable taxes, and a total.

Give the original to the customer and retain a copy for your records. These books are in numerical order and your accounting copy should be filed that way. The third copy stays in the book and is

MELANIE'S GIFT BASKETS (studio/office operation)
OPENING BALANCE SHEET
AS AT _____, 200-

ASSETS:

Petty cash	$50
Monies in bank	2,000
Inventory: baskets	2,500
supplies (including brochures)	6,050
Accounts receivable	0
Deposits	500
Prepaid expenses	1,300
Furniture and equipment	1,825
Computers and printer	4,000
TOTAL ASSETS	**$18,225**

LIABILITIES:

Sales tax payable	$0
Federal taxes payable	0
Accounts payable	4,000
Employee benefits payable	0
Wages payable	0
Monies owed to bank/investors	0

EQUITY:

Owner's investment in company	$14,225
Net profit/loss to date	0
TOTAL LIABILITIES AND EQUITY	**$18,225**

a backup record in case your file copy is misplaced. Remember to stamp the invoice paid.

2. Credit card sales

In addition to filling out the above invoice form you need to fill out the credit card receipt form. Make sure the date on your credit card imprinter is current. Run the card through the imprinter or fill in the information by hand if the customer is not present. Have the customer sign the credit card form and phone in for authorization if the amount is over your floor limit or if the customer is not present. Give the customer a copy of the credit card receipt and the invoice, or mail it to the customer if he or she is not present. Staple one copy of the credit card receipt to your file copy of the invoice and retain the hard copy of the credit card for deposit.

3. Invoiced sales

For sales transactions where you bill or invoice the customer, it is helpful to have an invoice on file in your company computer. A sample copy of this type of invoice is in chapter 7. After you have set up the invoice initially in your computer, always save the changes when you have generated a new invoice. Doing this allows you to keep track of the number sequence and to simply type over the data that you need to change. Send the original to the customer and retain one copy for your records. Keep the file copies of the invoices in a three-ring binder in numerical order and by month of transaction. Start a new binder for each fiscal year. You may also find it beneficial to make a copy to include in the customer's individual file. When you receive a check for the order, remember to stamp the invoice paid.

Set a designated time to input this information into your computer accounting system. You could schedule this duty on a daily basis, twice a week, or once a week for a longer period of time. Whenever you decide to schedule time to do computer data entry, make sure that you will not be distracted by the phone or other interruptions as it requires a high level of concentration.

Sales are put under the heading "Accounts Receivable" on your accounting system. If kept current, you will have a complete list of your customers, a contact name, an address, and phone and fax numbers. Your receivable account will also give you total sales for the month and let you know exactly what money was received in local and federal taxes. Keep your books current and consistently input the data to monitor how much money you may owe the government and what money is owed to you by customers.

Not declaring all sources of income from your business is tax fraud, and apart from being illegal, undeclared income will not be to your benefit if you are applying for a business loan or decide at some future time to sell your company. You cannot expect a reputable buyer or loan officer to take you seriously on the basis that your company is more profitable than the books show, because you cheat on your income tax.

d. Accounts Payable

Accounts payable generally fall under two categories: those purchases or expenses that relate directly to the cost of sales, and purchases or expenses necessary to operate your business. Cost of sales purchases are your baskets or containers, products you sell in the baskets, basket-making materials, freight in charges for those items, and freight out or delivery charges for your basket sales. Operating expenses payable are rent, utilities, wages, office supplies, memberships, advertising, promotions, postage, legal expenses, or other professional services etc. Accounts payable generally fall under one of the following five categories:

    (a) petty cash,

    (b) COD and cash purchases,

    (c) payable invoices,

    (d) company credit cards, and

    (e) personally paid company expenses.

1. Petty cash

Write a check to your bank for petty cash — $100 to $200 — and keep that money in a locked box or drawer to use for last minute or incidental expenses and to make change for cash sales. Buy a book of petty cash receipts and attach the sales slip from your purchases to the receipt. Write enough information on the form so you will know what expense account number it should go to when doing your computer accounting.

When the petty cash is almost gone, write another check to bring the amount up to the petty cash float you have decided to maintain. File the petty cash receipts in numerical order by month.

2. COD and cash purchases

As I have previously explained, it will probably be necessary for you to pay for many of your initial purchases on a cash-on-delivery basis. Pay for these purchases by company check and keep a copy of the invoice or sales receipt. Stamp your copy of the receipt paid, write the date of payment, the check number, as well as which expense account it should go to. Put these paid receipts into a file for the month they were paid and after you input the data into your computer accounting system (make sure you stamp them as having been entered). File them alphabetically or by supplier.

It will be very important for you to have easy access to these files in the future when you repeat orders or want to look up what something cost or how many you previously ordered.

3. Payable invoices

When you have set up an account with a supplier, they will invoice you and give you terms or dating. The terms will depend on what type of account you have set up or who the supplier is. The telephone company will expect the bill to be paid by a specific date. A basket supplier may give you 30 days. Paying your bills on time is essential to your long-term credit rating.

When you write a check for the invoice, mark it paid and put the date and check number on your file copy. Keep these invoices in a file for the month that they pertain to and then enter them to the proper account on your accounts payable computer accounting system. Mark them as having been entered and file them for easy future access.

4. Company credit cards

Having a credit card that you use solely for company business will help streamline your accounting and bookkeeping. There will be certain instances when paying with a credit card is your only option. It will be much less complicated if you use a credit card designated for business purchases only. Treat the bill the way you would any other payable invoice. Using a credit card is the normal way for paying for business travel and entertaining clients.

Keep good records if you intend to deduct these expenses from your income. Write as much information as possible on the back of your credit card receipt about the meeting or reason for the expense. Your accountant will be able to tell you what the allowable deduction is in your area for travel and entertainment expenses.

5. *Personally paid company expenses*

Purchase a book of employee expense account forms at your local stationery store. Use these forms for recording any out-of-pocket expenses you or any employees may incur. Make sure these expense reports are kept up to date and done every month.

Whenever possible, a receipt should be attached to the report; however, there are occasions when small amounts such as parking meters, gratuities, or automobile expenses may be reported without receipt backup. Write a company check to yourself or to your employees for the amount owing, record the date and check number on the expense form, and file it for input into the accounting system for the month that it pertains to.

Keep these expense reports filed in a separate place by month and by year. This is the type of backup you would be required to produce if your company was ever to be audited by the tax department. Both the IRS and Revenue Canada require that all vehicle expenses be recorded and kept. You must keep the entire year's expenses, including fuel, repairs, insurance, parking, depreciation, interest on the vehicle loan, and licensing and registration fees. If you use your vehicle for both business and pleasure, allocate the expense to your business based on a percentage of business to pleasure use. Your company accountant will be able to help you correctly allocate vehicle expenses to your business.

e. *Payroll*

If your company is incorporated or if you have employees, you are responsible for deductions at source from your employees' wages or salaries. You must open an account with your local tax department. You will be assigned a number and will receive a book of tables to use as reference for figuring out the deductions you must make each month, and the portion that you are required to pay for unemployment insurance or government pension plans.

Read the information carefully and phone or meet with a tax department representative if you have questions or are unsure of what is expected of you as an employer. It is your responsibility to file on time and correctly with any government entity. Your computer accounting system will have a separate heading called payroll and all payments and information regarding employment will be entered there. The person who teaches you the system will be able to show you everything you need to know regarding the use of the payroll account. Keep accurate payroll records in the event of any kind of dispute you may have with a current or former employee.

f. Inventory

Some of the most useful information you can receive from your computer accounting system is the tracking of inventory. Inputting your inventory purchases correctly into the computer saves time and gives a better financial picture.

You must have enough inventory on hand for future sales; that inventory needs to be put into a separate account for a true picture of your cost of sales and profitability at the end of each month.

For example, when you open your business and you place initial opening orders for product with a supplier, all of that stock would go into your accounting system under inventory. As you make and sell baskets during the month, those items that were sold would be moved from the inventory account to the cost of sales account relating to the baskets that you sold. Any leftover stock would then be carried forward into the next month's opening inventory account.

How detailed you want to get with inventory tracking will depend on the type of accounting program you use and the size of your business. A very detailed system would have a separate entry for each individual product or item that you carry. A more general inventory system would have a total amount of inventory by supplier or category. I use a very detailed inventory control system because I like to know exactly how much of each product I have on hand and I want a very accurate accounting of the profitability of my company on a monthly basis. By keeping your books current and up-to-date you should have a financial statement and balance sheet at the end of each month that gives you all of the following information for the month and for the year to date: gross sales, cost of sales, gross profit, expenses, net profit, payroll, payroll deductions due, federal taxes due, local taxes due, accounts receivable, accounts payable, inventory on hand, assets and liabilities.

g. Maximizing Deductible Expenses

It is very important that you keep track of all your expenses that may be deductible on your taxes. Expenses are allowed if they are related to the operation of the business, are reasonable, ordinary and necessary, and if they are for items to be used within a period of one year. Your accountant can advise you in your situation.

If you are going to incur expenses that would be useful for more than one year, generally that expense cannot be fully deducted within the year the money is spent. The depreciation formula for expenses such as computers, desks, automobiles, etc., may be claimed for the useful life of the asset.

One of the main advantages of running a home-based business is your right to deduct a certain portion of your home expenses, such as heat, rent, taxes, utilities, and mortgage. To take advantage of these deductions you must prove that you use a specific area of your home solely for the purpose of running your business. You cannot claim deductions for an office or workshop that also occupies a part of your kitchen or bedroom. Your accountant will be able to advise you as to what deductions are legal in your area. To ensure that you account for all expenses, keep all payment stubs, receipts, and vouchers, and maintain a record of entertainment and automobile expenses. The tax department can disallow claims for expenses if they are not verified.

Some of the areas you should discuss with your accountant are —

(a) home office (if applicable),

(b) automobile,

(c) entertainment,

(d) travel,

(e) bad debts,

(f) insurance,

(g) education and professional development,

(h) business association memberships,

(i) salaries (if you employ family members),

(j) equipment, and

(k) furnishings.

It is critical that you receive expert tax advice in advance on these and other expense deductions related to your business. Tax regulations and interpretations change frequently. Only a tax accountant can properly advise you on the appropriate deductions in your situation.

h. Accountants

Do not rely on the advice of a bookkeeper when it comes time to file your year-end and to pay taxes. Seek the advice and services of a professional accountant who can advise you on how to minimize tax payable and maximize your profits according to the most current rules and regulations. Again, tax rules and regulations are highly complex, vary according to your business location, and are constantly changing.

Trying to look after your own business accounting with no outside assistance is as foolish as trying to be your own doctor or lawyer. Sometimes you simply must pay for the advice and services of a professional.

Minimize the amount of work your accountant will have to do in order to finalize your books and file your taxes by updating your books each month and keeping properly organized records. Ask your lawyer, bank manager, or other business owner for the names of several accountants. Very large accounting firms are too expensive and will likely give your file to a junior accountant who has no clue about running a small business. An accountant in a small- to medium-size firm will probably be more affordable and will also have a greater understanding of your business.

Do not hesitate to interview several people before making your choice and ask up front about what kind of fees you can expect. A long-term relationship with an accountant can be very rewarding to your business, so hire someone you relate to on a personal level who can explain financial information in plain language.

Chapter 14

A FINAL WORD —
GROWTH AND
YOUR BUSINESS

After a year or two of success with your gift basket venture, you may want to consider expanding your operation. Following are some areas of expansion that are typical for a successful gift basket business to pursue and a brief discussion of the advantages and disadvantages.

a. Advertising Specialties or Promotional Merchandise

If you are dealing with corporate clients or clients who order large quantities of merchandise, it is likely that you will be asked to provide items that are imprinted with a logo or some type of custom wording. For example, a professional association that is holding its annual convention in New York might want you to print the association's logo with the words, "New York 1996" on a few items. These could be mugs, pens, ribbons, balloons, special containers, clothing items, chocolates, or food articles. The number of products available for customization is endless.

The method of imprinting can include silk screening, hot stamping, pad printing, laser printing, and embroidery, to name just a few. Each type of customization has special and specific requirements and is something that takes a great deal of care if it is to be done properly. These types of orders usually require you to meet specific deadlines and there isn't any room for errors or mistakes. If you start to get requests for custom merchandise, make sure you do your research and fully understand the imprinting process. Always ask for a proof of the art work and have your client sign it off before allowing the product to be imprinted. It only takes a slip of a few letters to make a big mistake. For example, there is a big difference in the meaning of the slogan "We Can Do It Better Together," and "We Can Do Better!" So do be sure to carefully proofread your copy and have someone else proof it along with your client or you could end up having to pay for a costly mistake as well as running the risk of losing a customer.

In North America, the Promotional Merchandise Association can give you access to many of the suppliers of this type of merchandise. However, it is not easy to join this association; it requires your proving that you have been doing that type of business for several years.

If this type of business interests you, I suggest that you start off by slowly learning as much as possible, first offering imprinted products that are easily obtainable, and then gradually growing into the business.

b. Gifts and Awards

An easier and more practical area for you to expand into is selling other gift merchandise. As you travel to gift shows, craft fairs, and other trade shows where products are sold wholesale, you will come into contact with many suppliers and artists who will have products appropriate for your clients.

There are many gift-giving occasions when gift baskets are not appropriate. If you have corporate clients they will be in need of gifts from time to time for speakers, employee recognition, visiting associates, retirements, distinguished directors of the board, etc. If you live in a community that has a large convention center or tourism industry, it is likely there are companies that offer welcome gifts or speakers' gifts to out-of-town visitors.

Look for products that can be engraved, or can have an engraved plaque attached to them or to the base, or that can be imprinted with a corporate name or the recipient's name. Look for products that are unique to your region or are made by local artisans.

The best way to find these people is to spend some time traveling around your region and attending art shows, craft fairs, and gallery openings. Word-of-mouth is also an excellent way to find hidden talent. Let your friends and associates know that you are in the market for unique and unusual items.

I don't think a week goes by that I am not contacted by an artist or craftsperson who is trying to market a product. Of course, some of these products may not be appropriate, but the vast majority are excellent and I always have new items on display in my showroom and to advertise in my mailings. This is important if you want to stay one step ahead of your competition and earn the reputation for always being able to find the perfect gift.

c. *Gift Basket Network*

If you live in an area with a cruise ship industry, you may be approached to become part of a network of companies that provide gifts on board the ships. The gift companies in other ports advertise that they provide gifts in your port location and you, in turn, advertise that you can provide gifts in other port locations. For example, if you are located in Los Angeles and you took an order for a gift leaving Miami, you would have to do the following:

(a) Fax the order to the Miami-based basket company and follow up with a phone call to make sure they received the order.

(b) Take payment from your client in Los Angeles.

(c) Follow up with another fax or phone call to make sure the gift was delivered on the sailing date.

(d) Deduct your commission from the payment and forward the rest to the Miami-based company.

(e) Hope that the quality and service provided by the Miami-based company is up to your standards.

Be very cautions before agreeing to this type of network operation. In order to make this type of arrangement worthwhile, the volume of orders coming into your port would need to be very high to justify your giving another company a cut of the profits, the costs incurred when phoning or faxing, and having to wait for payment.

My main concern with this type of arrangement is that you have no control over the product, service, or delivery. I know of several companies that have become involved in this type of business and lost loyal customers because the other companies in the network did not produce.

My company ships gifts and gift baskets all over the world and I do not think it is really necessary to become involved with a gift basket network. Many of the companies that do get involved with networks offer a very basic and mediocre product and that should not be the type of company you want to represent you. If you really are determined to expand your operation into another regional market, your time would be better spent opening up a branch of your existing operation in another area.

That being said, there really isn't anything too complicated about starting a gift basket company and the people you hire to run your other location could easily let you put in all the capital and effort and then start another operation with your customer base.

Expansion is often the downfall of many small businesses, so make sure you are ready before you get into any serious growth. Enjoy the success of the business you have, and move forward when you are ready.

Good luck!

APPENDIX
GIFT AND CRAFT SHOWS

Following is a list of gift and craft shows, venues, and organizers, listed alphabetically by city. Please note that information was current at the time of writing and is subject to change.

UNITED STATES

ATLANTA, GA

January and July

Atlanta International Area Rug Market
AmericasMart — Atlanta
AmericasMart

Atlanta International Gift and Home Furnishing Market
AmericasMart — Atlanta
AmericasMart

March

ACC Craft Show — Atlanta
Georgia Dome
American Craft Council

Atlanta Spring Gift, Accessories, and Holiday Market
AmericasMart — Atlanta
AmericasMart

Atlanta Trim-A-Tree/Christmas Show
Americasmart — Atlanta
AmericasMart

March and September

Atlanta National Gift and Decorative Accessories Market
AmericasMart — Atlanta
AmericasMart

May and October

Atlanta Immediate Delivery Show
AmericasMart — Atlanta
AmericasMart

September

Atlanta National Gourmet Show
AmericasMart — Atlanta
AmericasMart

ATLANTIC CITY, NJ

November

Atlantic City Souvenir and Resort Merchandise Show
The New Atlantic City Convention Center
Fairchild Urban Expositions

BALTIMORE, MD

February

ACC Craft Fair
Baltimore Convention Center
American Craft Council

BOSTON, MA

January, February, March, July, September, and October

The Center Gift Shows
The Bedford Center

March and August

Boston Gift Show
Bayside Exposition Center

March and September

Furniture and Decorative Accessory
Market of New England
Worcester Centrum Center

CHARLOTTE, NC

January, June, and August

Charlotte Gift Show
Charlotte Merchandise Mart
Charlotte Gift Show

December

ACC Craft Show — Charlotte
New Charlotte Convention Center
American Craft Council

CHICAGO, IL
January

NHMA International Housewares Show
McCormick Place
National Housewares Manufacturers Association

January, March, and July

Chicago Gift and Accessories Market
Chicago Merchandise Mart

Merchandise Mart Properties
TransWorld Housewares and Variety Exhibit
Rosemont Convention Center
TransWorld Exhibits

January and July

Beckman's Gift Show
Merchandise Mart Expo Center
Industry Productions of America

Chicago Gift Show
McCormick Place, Lakeside Center

March

Fancy Food Show — Spring
McCormick Place, Lakeside Center
National Association for the Specialty Food Trade

June

International Collectible Exposition
Rosemont Convention Center
McRand International

July

The ACCI Show
Rosemont Exposition Center
Association of Crafts and Creative Industries

COLUMBUS, OH
January to October

Columbus Gift Mart
Columbus Gift Mart

January, March, and August

Heritage Market Cash and Carry Wholesale Market
The Ramada Univeristy Inn
Heritage Productions

March and August

Columbus Gift Show
Columbus Convention Center
Fairchild Urban Expositions

March and August

Ohio State Gift Show
Veteran's Memorial Building
Offinger Management Company

DALLAS, TX
January, March, June, and September

Dallas National Gift and Decorative Accessories Market
Dallas Market Center
Dallas Market Center

Dallas Toy Show
Dallas Market Center
Dallas Market Center

January and June

Beckman's Gift Show
Dallas Market Hall
Industry Productions of America

Dallas National Bed, Bath, and Linen Show
Dallas Market Center
Dallas Market Center

March

Dallas Holiday Gift/Decorative Accessories Market
Dallas Market Center
Dallas Market Center

October

JPMA International Juvenile Product Show
Dallas Market Center
Juvenile Products Manufacturers Association

DENVER, CO
February and August

Denver Merchandise Mart Gift, Jewelry, and Resort Show
Denver Merchandise Mart
Denver Merchandise Mart

DETROIT, MI
January to November

Michigan Gift Mart Show
Michigan Gift Mart

EDISON, NJ
February and August

Mid-Atlantic Furniture and Accessory Market
New Jersey Convention and Expo Center
Karel Exposition Management

March and September

Heritage Cash and Carry Wholesale Market
New Jersey Convention, Raritan Center
Heritage Productions

April

    International Collectible Exposition
    New Jersey Convention and Expo Center
    McRand International

GATLINBURG, TN
March, June, September, and November

    Norton's Gatlinburg Gift and Variety Show
    Gatlinburg Convention Center
    The Norton Shows

GETTYSBURG, PA
May and November

    Heritage Cash and Carry Wholesale Market
    Eisenhower Inn and Conference Center
    Heritage Productions

HIGH POINT, NC
April

    High Point Decorative Accessories and Gift Mart
    114 N. Main Street, High Point, NC
    Fairchild Urban Expositions

April and October

    International Home Furnishings Market Association

HONOLULU, HI
January and September

    Hawaii Market: Apparel, Gift, Jewelry, and Fashion
      Accessories Show
    Blaisdell Exhibition Center
    Douglas Trade Shows

April and November

    Hawaii Market Cash and Carry Merchandise Expo
    Blaisdell Exhibition Center
    Douglas Trade Shows

INDIANAPOLIS, IN
January to November

    Indianapolis Gift Show
    Indianapolis Gift Mart

KANSAS CITY, KS
October

    Heritage Cash and Carry Wholesale Market
    Kansas City Gift Mart, International Trade Center
    Heritage Productions

KANSAS CITY, MO
January, March, June, July, and October

    Kansas City Gift Market

June

    Kansas City Country Market
    Kansas City Gift Mart
    Americana Sampler

LONG BEACH, CA
September

    Society of Craft Designers Educational Seminar
    Hyatt Regency Long Beach
    Society of Craft Designers

LOS ANGELES, CA
January, March, July, and September

    Los Angeles Mart Gift and Decorative Accessories and
      Furniture Market
    Los Angeles Mart

January and July

    Beckman's Gift Show
    Los Angeles Convention Center
    Industry Productions of America

    California Gift Show
    Los Angeles Convention Center
    DMG Exhibition Group Event

MEMPHIS, TN
January and August

    Memphis Gift and Jewelry Show
    Memphis-Cook Convention Center
    Helen Brett Enterprises

April and November

    Mid-South Jewelry and Accessories Fair
    Memphis-Cook Convention Center
    Helen Brett Enterprises

MIAMI, FL
January

    Miami International Gift and Decorative Accessories Show
    Miami International Merchandise Mart and
      Radisson Center
    Fairchild Urban Expositions

January and August

    Miami Gift Show
    Miami International Merchandise Mart and Radisson Center

MINNEAPOLIS, MN
January, March, June, August, and October

    Minneapolis Gift Show
    Minneapolis Gift Mart

October

    Society of Craft Designers Educational Seminar
    Hyatt Regency Minneapolis
    Society of Craft Designers

MYRTLE BEACH, SC
December

    Grand Strand Gift and Resort Merchandise Show
    Myrtle Beach Convention Center
    Fairchild Urban Expositions

NEW ORLEANS, LA
January and August

    New Orleans Gift and Jewelry Show
    Ernest N. Morial Convention Center
    Helen Brett Enterprises

NEW YORK, NY
January, May, and August

    Fashion Accessories Expo
    Jacob K. Javits Convention Center
    Ullo International Exhibition Group

January and August

    New York Gift Market at 225
    The Gift Building

    New York Gift Show
    230 Fifth Avenue Market Center
    Newmark and Co. Real Estate

February

    American International Toy Fair
    Participating showrooms
    Toy Manufacturers of America

    Toy Fair/Trim-A-Tree
    230 Fifth Avenue Market Center
    Newmark and Co. Real Estate

February, June, September, and November

    General Merchandise Market
    230 Fifth Avenue Market Center
    Newmark and Co. Real Estate

February, April, June, July, and September

    The Merchandise Shows
    Miller Freeman

February and August

    New York Gift Show at Forty-One Madison
    New York Merchandise Mart

    New York International Gift Fair, Including: Accent on
      Design, Just Kidstuff, and the Museum Source
    Jacob K. Javits Convention Center and Passenger
    Ship Terminal

April and October

    Extracts — A Trade Show for Aromatherapy,
      Home Fragrance, and Personal Care
    Jacob K. Javits Convention Center

April and September

    New York Home Textiles Market Week
    230 Fifth Avenue Market Center
    Newmark and Co. Real Estate

April and September

    New York Tabletop Market
    230 Fifth Avenue Market Center
    Newmark and Co. Real Estate

May

    National Stationery Show
    230 Fifth Avenue Market Center
    Newmark and Co. Real Estate

    Premium Incentive Show
    Jacob K. Javits Convention Center
    Bill Comm Exposition and Conference Group

    Surtex
    Jacob K. Javits Convention Center

June

    Licensing 99 International
    Jacob K. Javits Convention Center
    Expocon, a division of Advanstar Communication

    Licensing International Show
    The Internationl Licensing and Merchandising
    Conference, Exposition, and Annual Meeting
    Advanstar Communications, Entertainment Group

July

    Fancy Food Show (NAFST) Summer
    Jacob K. Javits Convention Center
    National Association for the Specialty Food Trade

September

    National Merchandise Show
    Jacob K. Javits Convention Center
    Miller Freeman

NIXA, MD
February

    Heart of America Gift Show

ORLANDO, FL
February

   Florida Gift Show Orlando
   Orange County Convention Center
   AmericasMart

February

   Florida Gift Show
   Orlando Convention Center
   AMC Gift Division Marketing

July

   Florida International Gift Show
   Orange County Convention Center
   Fairchild Urban Expositions

August

   Florida International Gift Show
   Orange County Convention Center
   Ullo International Exhibition Group

September

   Orlando Furniture and Decorative Accessory Market
   Orange County Convention Center
   Karel Exposition Management

PHILADELPHIA, PA
January and July

   Philadelphia Gift Show
   Fort Washington Expo Center
   Fairchild Urban Expositions

   Buyers Market of American Craft
   Pennsylvania Convention Center
   The Rosen Group

PHOENIX, AZ
February and August

   Oasis Gift Show
   Phoenix Civic Plaza
   OASIS

PITTSBURGH, PA
January and August

   Pittsburgh Gift Show
   Pittsburgh Expo Mart
   American Gift and Art Shows

PORTLAND, OR
January and June

   Portland Gift Show
   Oregon Convention Center
   Western Exhibitors

ROCHESTER, NY
February and July

   Western New York Gift Show
   The Dome Center
   American Gift and Art Shows

SALT LAKE CITY, UT
February and August

   Salt Lake Gift Show
   Salt Palace Convention Center
   Progressive Exhibitors

SAN FRANCISCO, CA
January

   Fancy Food Show — Winter
   Moscone Convention Center
   National Association for the Specialty Food Trade

January and August

   San Francisco International Gift Fair
   Moscone Center
   Western Exhibitors

May

   Gourmet Products Show
   Ernest J. Morial Convention Center, New Orleans, LA

August

   ACC Craft Fair — San Francisco
   Fort Mason Center
   American Craft Council

SARASOTA, FL
December

   ACC Craft Show — Sarasota
   Robarts Arena
   American Craft Council

SEATTLE, WA
January and August

   Seattle Gift Show
   Seattle Center
   Western Exhibitors

ST. PAUL, MN
April

   ACC Craft Show — St. Paul
   River Center
   American Craft Council

TAMPA, FL
December

ACC Craft Show — Sarasota
Roberts Arena
American Craft Enterprises

TUCSON, AZ
February

HBE Gem and Jewelry Show
Tucson Exposition Center Marketplace USA
Helen Brett Enterprises

VALLEY FORGE, PA
February and June

Heritage Cash and Carry Wholesale Market
Heritage Productions

Heritage Market of American Crafts
The Hilton Hotel
Heritage Productions

Heritage Market of Distinguished Artisans
The Holiday Inn
Heritage Productions

WASHINGTON, DC
January, March, April, June, July, September, and October

Greater Washington Gift Mart Show
Washington Gift Mart

January and July

Washington Gift Show
Capital Expo Center

WEST SPRINGFIELD, MA
April and July

Heritage Cash and Carry Wholesale Market
Better Living Center, Eastern State Expo
Heritage Productions

CANADIAN MARKETS

MISSISSAUGA, ON
January

Toronto International Home Furnishings Market
International Center
Quebec Furniture Manufacturers Association

MONTREAL, QC
March and August

Montreal Gift Show
Place Bonaventure
Southex Exhibitions

May and October

Giftware Markets
Place Bonaventure
Place Bonaventure

September

Montreal Furniture Market
Place Bonaventure
Quebec Furniture Manufacturers Association

NORTHLANDS, AB
February and August

Alberta Gift Show
Northlands Agricom
Southex Exhibitions

TORONTO, ON
January and August

CGTA Gift Show
International Center, Toronto Congress Center
Canadian Gift and Tableware Association

Mode Accessories Show
International Plaza Hotel and Conference Center
Two Plus One Group

February

Toronto Gift Show
National Trade Center, Exhibition Place
Southex Exhibitions

April

Canadian Luggage, Leather Goods, Handbags, and
     Accessories Show
International Center
Pro-Sho

VANCOUVER, BC
March and September

Vancouver Gift Show
BC Place Stadium
Southex Exhibitions

WILLOWDALE, ON
June

Paperex 99
Metear Show Productions

GLOSSARY

ACCOUNTS RECEIVABLE

The record used to account for sales made through the extension of credit

ADVERTISING SPECIALITIES

Products that are designed to have a corporate identity or logo imprinted, hot stamped, silk screened, or embroidered on them

AGENT

A manufacturer's representative who sells one or more lines of merchandise at wholesale

BALANCE SHEET

A monthly financial statement used to report the total assets, liabilities, and equity of a business

CASH ON DELIVERY (COD)

Term for cash payment on receipt of goods until credit is established

COST PER THOUSAND (CPM)

Term used in media buying that refers to the cost it takes to reach a thousand people within your target market

DEMOGRAPHICS

Population statistics categorized by age, income, sex, education, and occupation that best describe your target market

DEPRECIATION

The decrease in value of fixed assets that provides the foundation of a tax deduction

DISTRIBUTOR

A company that markets products for a variety of manufacturers at a slightly higher than wholesale price

DOING BUSINESS AS (DEA)

A fictitious company name used by sole proprietors or partnerships, under which the business operates

FIXED EXPENSES

Monthly expenses that do not fluctuate with the sales volume (e.g., rent)

FREIGHT ON BOARD (FOB)

The destination point where the purchaser of goods is responsible for the cost of shiping. For example, if you live in New York and order goods that are FOB Los Angeles, you are responsible for the freight charge from Los Angeles to New York

INCOME STATEMENT

A monthly statement charting the sales and operating costs of a business

KEYSTONE

A term used in retail, meaning the doubling of the cost of product

MANUFACTURER

The direct source of a manufactured product

MARKET SURVEY

A research method used to define the potential market for a business

MARK-UP

The amount added to the cost of goods in order to attain the desired profit

NET PROFIT ON SALES

The measure of profitability that determines the difference between net profit and operating expenses

OVERHEAD

All nonlabor expenses needed to operate a business

PROFIT

Generally, there are two types of profits: gross and net. Gross profit is the difference between gross sales and cost of sales. Net profit is the difference between gross profit and all costs associated with operating a business

VARIABLE EXPENSES

Business costs that can fluctuate from month to month according to the sales volume

WHOLESALER

A merchant who sells goods primarily to retailers or commercial users mainly for resale or business use